How to
Make
Love
to a
Lobster

How to Make Love to a Lobster

An Eclectic Guide to the Buying, Cooking, Eating and Folklore of Shellfish

Fitzhenry & Whiteside

MARJORIE HARRIS and PETER TAYLOR

Fitzhenry & Whiteside,
195 Allstate Parkway,
Markham, Ontario L3R 4T8

In the United States,
121 Harvard Avenue, Suite 2,
Allston, Massachusetts 02134

www.fitzhenry.ca   godwit@fitzhenry.ca

Fitzhenry & Whiteside acknowledges with thanks the Canada Council for the Arts,
the Government of Canada through the Book Publishing Industry Development Program (BPIDP),
and the Ontario Arts Council for their support for our publishing program.

10   9   8   7   6   5   4   3   2   1

National Library of Canada Cataloguing in Publication

Harris, Marjorie
How to make love to a lobster : an eclectic guide to
the buying, cooking, eating and folklore of shellfish /
Marjorie Harris and Peter Taylor.

First ed. published: Toronto : Macmillan of Canada, 1988.

ISBN 1-55041-761-4

1. Cookery (Shellfish)   2. Shellfish.   I. Taylor, Peter
II. Title.

TX753.H37 2003   641.6'94   C2003-900910-6

U.S. Publisher Cataloging-in-Publication Data
(Library of Congress Standards)

Harris, Marjorie.
How to make love to a lobster : an eclectic guide to
the buying, cooking, eating and folklore of shellfish /
Marjorie Harris and Peter Taylor.
[150] p. :   cm.
Summary: Fact, folklore, history and trivia about
shellfish; includes recipes from seafood restaurants
in the United States and Canada.
ISBN 1-55041-761-4   (pbk.)
1. Shellfish.   2. Cookery (Shellfish).   I. Taylor, Peter.
II. Title.
641.394 21   TX387.H31 2003

Cover design by: Darrell McCalla
Cover photo: Dick Loek
Cover photo lobster supplied by: Bill's Lobster / Toronto
Interior design and typesetting by: Daniel Crack, Kinetics Design
Printed and bound in Canada

Contents

List of Favorite Recipes

List of Favorite Recipes

Preface and Acknowledgments

The idea for this book bubbled around our conversations for a long time as we reminisced, from time to time, about meals which were memorable because they became great sensual occasions. We wanted to read more about shellfish but, since it was difficult to find everything we wanted to know in one place, we felt that writing this book would fill an aching gap, not only for us but also for all those who enjoy shellfish as much as we do.

Devotees will tell you that eating these wonderful beasts is not only healthy but also very sexy. They insist there has to be some truth to the many myths that expound their aphrodisiac qualities and more than one reason why so many of them have been immortalized in numerous stories, poems and songs.

Our primordial ancestors must have instinctively known that shellfish were not only good for the soul but also life sustaining. Having crawled from the ocean, one theory has it, our forebears remained seaside, feeding their brains on a diet of marine creatures for the roughly 10,000 years that it took them to learn to stand erect and head downtown. As modern science continued to uncover more and more secrets about them, we too learned to appreciate the nutritional value. We got to like mussels and scallops because they were low in cholesterol and easily absorbed by the body. We found out why oysters and shrimps did wonders for our sex lives and why squid and octopus, although rich in proteins, would not make us fat.

Apart from these "sensible" qualities of shellfish, we also discovered that no other food made us feel quite as nostalgic. As we strolled through our separate pasts, we were suddenly reminded that the clams we dug on a Cape Cod beach and that the freshly picked oysters enjoyed on Malpeque Bay meant more to us than simply stopping for a roadside snack on a summer day.

In compiling the information for this book, we are greatly indebted to the many writers who went before us and to those whose material we quote in the book: James Beard, Hector Bolitho, Lewis Carroll, Rebecca Charles; Deborah DiClementi; Euell Gibbons, Anne Hardy, Arthur Hawkins, Jan Haworth, Robert Hendrickson, Sarah Hurlburt, Hsian Ju Lin, Tsuifeng Lint, A. J. McClane, Jill Nhu Huong Miller, D. R. Percy, Waverly Root, John G. Saxe, A. R. Scammell, Eva Jean Schulz, George Sterling, Bonnie Stern, Herb Taylor, William W. Warner and C. M. Yonge.

Although we have done our best to contact everyone to ask for permission to use the material included in the book, we apologize to those we were unable to reach, hoping to rectify any credit omissions before the next edition is published.

We are grateful to the many friends and "foodies" who gave us ideas and supplied the names of their favorite seafood restaurants. (They are mentioned by name at the beginning of the Appendix — "Good Places to Eat Shellfish"). Special thanks go to the chefs who kindly permitted us to reprint their best shellfish recipes: John Canepa, Pia Carroll, Rebecca Charles, Patrick Desmoulins, Kee Lee, Chris McNulty and Michael Stadtlander.

We also would like to express our appreciation to Tony Aspler, author of *Tony Aspler's International Guide to Wine, The Wine Lover Dines* (with Master Chef Jacques Marie) and *Vintage Canada*, who compiled for us an impressive list of wines to accompany the various shellfish dishes.

Marjorie Harris and Peter Taylor

The Elegant Lobster

"You don't simply eat a lobster –
you make love to it!"

No other words have ever so poignantly expressed the intimacy this remarkable crustacean evokes, regardless whether they were spoken by a passionate gourmand or by an individual engaged in wiping melted butter off his or her lover's chin. What other food demands so many skills? What other meal invites you to come so close to your plate? No other dish can make the juices of romance flow quite as swiftly. You can eat it boiled, steamed, poached, or broiled — on the beach at sunset or in the privacy of your hot tub; sitting in your favorite restaurant, you can even have it served flambéed with Pernod!

To look at a lobster's physical attributes you'd never guess why it is consumed with such gusto. Resembling a science fiction writer's dream come true, this armored, ten-legged denizen of the deep is, nonetheless, prized by gourmets the world over.

Lobsters weighing upward of forty pounds have been caught; they have been known to get fifty years old — some even one hundred — although scientists say their ages are difficult to determine. They shed their shells as often as twenty-four times in a seven-year period and when they lose a claw they can regrow it the next time they change shells. The stalk of a lobster's eye contains a growth-inhibiting hormone; for some strange reason, when blinded, it grows twice as fast as its sighted relatives.

North Americans love *homarus Americanus* or, simply, the American Lobster. It is found along the eastern seaboard — from Labrador to North Carolina — and the fact that it is known as "Maine," "New England," "Atlantic," "Nova Scotia," "New Brunswick," "Prince Edward Island," or "Newfoundland" lobster, has more to do with those regions' public relations efforts than with actual differences in taste.

Regardless where in North America it comes from, it is its two large pincers which distinguish the American Lobster from its clawless cousin the Spiny Lobster. It inhabits not only the rocky bottoms of European coastal waters, but also is found off the coasts of Florida and California and in the Gulf of Mexico. The succulent flesh inside the American's claws makes it the undisputed king of all the crustaceans. Like no other seafood, it can be relied upon always to turn heads as it makes its way across countless dining rooms — preferably on silver platters — to the tables of discriminating diners.

It Was Not Always Thus ...

Before 1800, lobsters were used as bait by North American fishermen. In some areas, they even were fed to pigs. References to their use as fertilizer for the fields and gardens of early northeast coast settlers can be found in more than one history book, even if historians and marine experts dismiss such data as apocryphal pioneer folklore. Lobsters were once so abundant in North America that they were called "the poor man's lunch." It is written that what most depressed the sixty-seven hardy souls, who landed at Plymouth Rock in 1622 was the fact that there was little else to eat but lobster!

Times Have Changed ...

Today, the universal demand for the American Lobster is at an all time high. Although in Canada and in the United States the value of the annual catch is conservatively estimated at half a billion dollars, populations have decreased and are threatened in certain areas. Existing stocks must be carefully monitored and protected by rotating harvesting seasons.

Using unlicensed traps to "poach" lobsters as well as stealing lobster-pots carries stiff penalties in North America. These pots are jealously guarded by fishermen who frequently are helped by a network of friends and neighbors living along the shore. Many a vacationing "sport" or recreational boatsman rues the day he found himself surrounded by angry lobstermen, only too willing to make a citizen's arrest until the police arrived.

There also are strict limits on the lengths and weights of lobsters that commercial fishermen can catch. In the cold waters of the Atlantic, they take approximately seven years to reach 1 1/4 to 1 1/2 pounds. Because as few as one in one thousand reach this market size in the oceans, aquaculture — lobster farming — has become a sensible alternative. Marine scientists tell us that in that environment, they can be raised from the larva stage to adulthood in just two years. However, until the system becomes commercially more viable, we must continue to rely on Neptune as our main source of supply. Fortunately, he has more than a little help from the prolific female crustacean.

Adult lobsters cover distances of up to 500 kilometers (300 miles) as they move about the ocean floor to feed and breed. After a single mating, the female saves enough of her mate's sperm to fertilize two or three broods of eggs over the next several years. She carries her eggs — as many as 5,000 – 50,000 — externally, on the feathery swimmerets located on the underside of her tail. Once hatched, her babies don't even look like lobsters, as they swim, float and feed for three to six weeks on the water surface before dropping down to the ocean floor.

How to Buy Lobsters

Go for the scrappiest and the most ornery of the lot. The slapping of the tail and the waving of claws and legs are its way of telling you, "I'm fresh and healthy."

Many gourmets buy only female lobsters, in the hope of finding them heavy with coral — the internal roe. These same people also claim that the female's meat is sweeter than that of the male.

How can you tell the difference between the sexes? On the underside of the lobster's tail are five pairs of feathery swimmerets; on the male, the first set, closest to the body, will be bony, hard and grooved, whereas it is soft, feathery and frequently crossed on the female.

Before buying cooked lobster, have your fishmonger unbend the beast's tail or ask to do it yourself. If it was fresh, healthy, and at it's best when cooked live, the tail will snap back into a curl. If it doesn't, ask for another one and, should your fish dealer argue the point, find another dealer.

Lobsters minus one claw are called "culls." They often are sold at special prices and, although this may make them attractive, they will yield less good meat per pound compared to the regular-priced, two-clawed variety.

How to Store Lobsters

A lobster can live more than one day out of the water and, when bought live, will keep safely up to a day in your refrigerator. Let it sit on a bed of seaweed but never store it directly on ice or in fresh water. Even if it dies overnight in the refrigerator, it still can be cooked the next day, as long as it was lively when you first bought it.

Lobsters purchased cooked in their shell, will keep up to three days in your refrigerator. Freeze cooked lobster meat in a brine made by mixing two teaspoons of salt with one cup of water. Stored in freezer containers, a lobster will keep up to two months in your freezer, set at zero degrees. To thaw, place it in the bottom, lower part of your refrigerator overnight.

Never re-freeze lobster meat!

How to Cook Lobsters

The persistent rumor that those exceeding 1 1/4 to 1 1/2 pounds are tough when cooked, is definitely not true. The larger ones are every bit as tender and sweet.

Observe recommended cooking times carefully, as overcooked lobster will be tough and chewy.

For brighter red shells, when boiling, steaming or poaching lobster, add three caps-full of vinegar to the water.

Boiling

Although the methods for boiling lobster vary, we prefer the following recommended by The Grand Central Oyster Bar in New York's Grand Central Station and by the authors of *The Joy of Cooking*.

Lobsters are best boiled live in sea water, but if you are nowhere near the sea, fill your lobster pot with enough water to completely cover the beasts, adding one teaspoon of salt for each quart of water. Bring to a rolling boil, then plunge the lobster, head first, into the water. If you are squeamish about this procedure, kill it first by severing the spinal cord with a sharp knife inserted between body and tail.

Let the water return to a second boil, cover the pot and reduce the heat immediately. Simmer the lobster for five minutes for the first pound and three minutes for each additional pound.

Steaming

Steaming is preferred by people who say that the lobster takes on water when it is boiled and that boiling toughens the meat.

Fill the pot with salt water to a depth of approximately 2 inches. When it begins to boil rapidly, stand the lobster, head first, in the steaming brew, cover, and cook twenty minutes (for a 1 1/2 pound lobster).

Poaching

This recipe, credited to the folks behind Time-Life Books' *The Good Cook* series, is widely touted by those who say that neither boiling nor steaming can match the tenderness achieved when the lobster is poached or gently simmered.

Bring to a slow simmer enough ocean or salted water to cover the lobster. Immerse it, head first, allowing approximately ten minutes for the water to return to the simmering point. Recommended cooking time: about twenty-five minutes per pound.

For a special taste treat, boiled, steamed or poached lobster can be placed shell-side-up on a barbecue for five minutes before serving.

Broiling

Kill the lobster by severing the spinal cord with a sharp knife inserted between body and tail. Place it on its back and slit it open from head to tail.

Remove the stomach sac (near the head) and the intestinal vein that runs down the middle of the tail. Reserve the tomalley and the roe.

Lay the two halves flat.

Mix tomalley and roe with breadcrumbs and a teaspoon of lemon juice. Tuck the mixture into the body cavity.

Brush the meat and stuffing with melted butter to which the juice of half a lemon has been added. Place the lobster, meat-side up, under a preheated broiler for about fifteen minutes.

How, O How Do You Eat the Beast?

Faced with this orange-scarlet crustacean for the very first time, you'll want to know how to go about removing the chunks of meat from the inside of the shell. Simple — with your hands!

While some people prefer to start with the claws, saving the tail to last, the choice is entirely up to you. In many restaurants, lobsters arrive at the table with the claws cracked and the tail split. If the task is left up to you, you will be provided with the appropriate utensils — scissor-like snippers for cutting the tail and an ordinary nutcracker for cracking the claws.

With your left hand, grasp the lobster firmly by its back or "saddle." Separate the tail from the body with a strong twisting motion of your right hand. In the same way, remove the claws, as well as the "arms" — the skinny part between the claws and the body. (You may want to protect your hand with a napkin as these spiny arms are very prickly.) Lastly, remove the "thumbs" from the claws by bending them back until they snap.

If the lobster has come to your table with the claws partially split, they will readily snap along the crack. Use the nutcracker, if they are still intact. Either way, the meat inside each claw half is easily removed with a fork.

The arms can be broken apart by hand at the knuckles or joints. Using a pick or fork, scoop out the meat from either end. However, few tools are better than your index or baby finger for pushing it through the small openings. The tiny morsels of meat in the thumbs can be removed with the pick or with a single tine of your fork.

To remove the meat from the lobster's tail, snap off the fan-like fins first and then push the fork firmly into the open end. By bending the tail backward in the opposite direction to which it curls, it, generally, is easier to snap it in half across the grain. Some people like to get at the meat with a forceful, steady pull, while others prefer to split the tail lengthwise, cutting it down the middle of the underside with the snippers. Then, using the strength of their wrists, and hands, they snap the tall in half along the split. The sweet meat inside the fins can be sucked and chewed out by using your front teeth as pincers.

Many people are more than a little intimidated by the lobster's body. Having devoured the claws and the tail, dipped in melted butter, they are reluctant to tackle anything that looks so impenetrable and stares back at them from the plate. A pity — for the body contains many treats.

First, there is the tomalley — the lobster's liver — to which some people disdainfully refer as "the green stuff." It is, however, popular enough to be featured as a bar appetizer at many oyster bars and, like goose liver paté, is a delicacy to be enjoyed on its own or spread on a cocktail cracker.

You'll find the roe — "the red stuff" to the uninitiated — inside a female lobster's body cavity. It is so favored by some that, for its sake alone, they will select or demand to be served only females when dining out.

To further explore the lobster's body, pretend you have before you a sports car with its hood hinged at the front, behind the headlights or eyes. Holding the body in your right hand — fingers under the belly, thumb inside — lift off the hood with your left hand. Done properly, the "crop" or gravel sac in the head should come away at the same time. Discard together with the hood or saddle shell.

Remove the spindly walking legs — there should be eight — which contain tiny, tasty bits of meat. Working backward from "foot" to "hip," they can be chewed out with your front teeth.

The U-shaped husk that remains on your platter is frequently discarded by restaurant diners. "A shame!" say those who have taken the trouble to find the nuggets of meat this "rib cage" contains. If you crave one more nibble, here is what you do:

Using your hands, break the body lengthwise along the breastbone by bending back the sides. Now prod, bend and dig with your fingertips in the thickest part of the two halves resting on your plate. The morsels you find may be as small as a peanut or as large as an oyster cracker.

While you dine, remove the shells from your plate, making certain that they are empty. Most restaurants provide a large bowl for this purpose and you might do the same when serving lobster at home.

Also remember that your guests will emerge from the feast cleaner, less sticky and more comfortable if you supply them with finger bowls. Restaurants usually do but if they don't be sure to ask for them.

Recipes

Lobster Americaine
The Whistling Oyster, Toronto   Courtesy: Chef Kee Lee
Serves 4

Sauce
6 tbsp	butter
6 tbsp	olive oil
3	bunches green onions, white part only, chopped
4 – 5	cloves garlic, crushed
16 – 20	fresh basil leaves, chopped or 2 tsp dried sweet basil
3	sprigs fresh thyme or 1 tsp dried thyme
1	bay leaf
3/4 lb	ripe tomatoes peeled, seeded and chopped
5 tbsp	tomato paste
1 cup	clam juice
1/4 cup	white wine (dry)
	salt and pepper to taste

Lobster
4	cooked lobsters, 1 1/4 – 1 1/2 lb each
6 tbsp	olive oil
1/2 cup	brandy
2 cups	white wine (dry)
Garnish	cayenne pepper
	lobster coral and liver (tomalley)

10

To make the sauce, melt butter in a large saucepan. Add olive oil and onions. Sauté for a few minutes. Add garlic, basil, thyme, bay leaf, tomatoes, tomato paste, clam juice and wine. Simmer for at least sixty minutes or until the sauce is thick and well blended. Season with salt and pepper.

While the sauce cooks, cut the lobsters in half. Reserve the coral and the liver (tomalley). Crack the claws and extract the meat. Cut the meat removed from the tail portion into three to four pieces.

In a large skillet, heat olive oil. Add the lobster pieces and sauté for a few minutes, turning quickly. Add wine and brandy then stir in the sauce. Simmer for twenty minutes.

Before serving the *Lobster Americaine* sprinkle with cayenne pepper and, at the last minute, add the reserved coral and liver, blending them thoroughly into the sauce.

Serve over freshly cooked Spinach Fettuccini.

Recipes

Lobster à la Newburg
Serves 4

2 cups	lobster meat, cut up
2 tbsp	butter
1 tsp	salt
1/4 tsp	cayenne pepper
1/4 tsp	nutmeg
2	egg yolks
1/2 cup	cream
3 tbsp	dry sherry
4	puff pastry shells

Melt the butter in a frying pan. Add the meat, salt, cayenne pepper and nutmeg and sauté over a low flame.

Beat the egg yolks into the cream. Add the mixture to the pan. Then gently but steadily stir in the sherry.

When the sauce begins to thicken, transfer the lobster to the pastry shells and serve.

Recommended Wines

European

Pinot Grigio
White Burgundy
Chardonnay
Sancerre Soave
Pouilly-Fume
Orvieto

North American

Chardonnay
Riesling (dry)
Sauvignon Blanc
Seyval Blanc
Fume Blanc

Vidal (dry)

Favorite Recipes

Lobster Rolls
Pearl Oyster Bar, New York

	The meat of a 1 pound lobster, per person (preferably culls*)
1/2	rib celery, chopped very finely
1/4 cup	mayonnaise
squeeze	of lemon
pinches	of salt and pepper
2	top loading hot dog buns

Rough chop the lobster meat into 1/2 in to 3/4 in pieces and put in a bowl with the rest of the ingredients. Mix until thoroughly combined. Cover and store this lobster salad in refrigerator until you need it.

People who claim they'd leap through burning hoops for a feed of lobster, say no visit to New England or Atlantic Canada is complete without stopping at every opportunity to sample the lobster rolls along the way. And while the presentation may vary slightly from establishment to establishment, the following recipe from Pearl Oyster Bar in New York's Greenwich Village is as close to perfect as this treat gets.

Melt 2 tsp sweet butter on low-medium heat in a small saucepan. Place hot dog buns on their sides in the butter. Flip buns over a couple of times so that both sides soak up an equal amount of butter and brown evenly.

When ready to dine, fill the buns with the lobster salad and top it off with a sprinkle of fresh chopped chives. The Pearl's chef and owner, Rebecca Charles is also the co-author (with Deborah DiClementi) of *Lobster Rolls and Blueberry Pie: Three Generations of Recipes and Stories from Summers on the Coast of Maine*. Her recommendation: serve your lobster rolls with shoestring fries and a garnish of baby greens.

* Culls, lobsters missing one or both of their claws, are cheaper. (Stay away from pre-cooked lobster meat which is generally overcooked, probably not fresh and definitely over-priced.)

The Elegant Lobster

13

Consider the Crab

"Laying right on the ice kills your soft crab dead;
too cold on the truck, same thing."

— From Beautiful Swimmers *by William W. Warner*

Marine biologists tell us that there are so many species of crab on our ocean floors that an enterprising restaurateur could create a menu featuring well over one thousand different kinds. Imagine trying to decide which one to try during an ordinary business luncheon!

It is anyone's guess whether the subtle nuances in taste and texture go hand in hand with the more noticeable differences in size and shape. However, there probably are enclaves of shellfish lovers who, at this very moment, are busily trying to discover just that.

The crab is a shellfish with four pairs of legs, one pair of claws, and a short, broad body folded under its chest. Like the lobster, it must shed its shell to grow but, unlike the lobster, cannot mate before molting or shedding its shell. Therefore, the female of the species must literally strip completely before the deed gets done.

The male crab, having reached what in human terms might be referred to as "the age of reason," tiptoes sideways along the ocean floor in search of love. When he spots the crab of his dreams about to disrobe, he quickly scoops her up in his arms and carries her off to a safe and private place. Here, protected from predators, she performs her awkward, slow striptease and the business of mating gets under way. Male Alaska King Crabs have been observed during the ritual engaging in what only can be described as rapacious foreplay, bouncing their mates along the ocean floor in an attempt to speed up the shedding process.

From the East Coast of North America comes the Atlantic Blue Crab and, from more northerly waters, the Queen or Snow Crab, largely used for canning. Most popular and almost synonymous with the State of Florida, is the Southern Stone Crab. On the west coast, the delectable Dungeness has long been the official good will ambassador of the Pacific.

The habitat of the Alaska King Crab ranges over a broad sweep of sub arctic ocean front — from the north end of Vancouver Island to the edge of the Bering Sea. The areas which are commercially most valuable lie off the Alaska Coast Peninsula, near the Aleutians, around Kodiac Island and in Cook Inlet.

Unlike the Blue Crab of the Atlantic or the Dungeness of the Pacific, the Alaska King Crab can grow to heroic proportions. While the largest on record is said to have had a leg spread of about five feet, weighing almost twenty-five pounds, ten-pound specimens measuring three feet across are not uncommon.

While the Alaska King Crab's body meat is utilized by canneries, the tender and delicious meat inside its long, spindly legs is so highly prized that even in regions where beef is king, crab legs have become a staple item in the "seafood" section of most North American restaurant menus.

Fully grown, Atlantic Blue Crabs measure five to seven inches across their carapace or shell, weighing one quarter to one pound each. While the tops of their claws are blue, they also can be identified by the unique way the top shell extends into a spike on each side, as well as by the thin red line that runs along the edges of their "paddlers" — a crab's rear legs.

Blue Crabs about to shed their shells are called "peelers" by the fishermen who harvest them. Since they cannot catch them while soft, they take them just before they reach their molting stage and hold them in boxes or floating pens until the actual peeling begins. At this point, the shells are soft, but before the new ones can become even paper thin, the crabs are quickly removed from the water and shipped to markets across the country and around the world. In their soft-shell state, they are graded by shell widths as follows:

Mediums	–	3 1/2 inches	to	4 inches
Hotels	–	4 "	to	4 1/2 "
Primes	–	4 1/2 "	to	5 "
Jumbos	–	5 "	to	5 1/2 "
Whales	–	5 1/2 "	and over	

The molting season for *callinectes sapidus* — the Atlantic Blue Crab — begins in spring when the coastal waters of the ocean warm to above sixty degrees. *Callinectes* is Greek for "beautiful swimmer," and *sapidus* is Latin for "savory," as in tasty and, therefore, good to eat.

As if these beautiful swimmers were not famous enough in their hard-shell state as a source of most of America's fresh crab meat. Each year, early in May, gourmands in the Chesapeake Bay area, joyfully hail the arrival of the soft shells as it is announced with great fanfare in the restaurants, fish markets and shellfish bars of Virginia and Maryland.

This celebration is particularly phenomenal, given the fact that of the more than 600 million blue crabs taken each year along America's eastern seaboard, a mere three per cent go to market in the soft-shell state. In late August, when cool water temperatures signal the end of the molting season, the feast is over, all too soon, as anyone with even half a taste bud will tell you.

Although the Chesapeake Bay area supplies virtually all the soft-shell Atlantic Blue Crabs to the world, hard-shells are found from Massachusetts to the northerly reaches of South America. However, commercially, they are most important in the region between Delaware and Florida and, again, in the Chesapeake Bay area of Virginia and Maryland where as many as one hundred "crab houses" or "picking plants" process their delicious meat throughout the season.

Canadians do not celebrate the crab with anything near the same enthusiasm as their American neighbors do. Some claim it is simply a matter of national taste in a country so well served by the lobsters from its North Atlantic waters, while others maintain that it is because crabbing is a much younger industry in Canada. Begun in the late 1960s and largely based on the supply of Snow and Queen Crabs found off the coast of Newfoundland and in the Gulf of St. Lawrence, most all of the Canadian catch is processed for export.

How to Cook Hard-Shell Crabs

Like lobsters, these crabs should be aggressive and snappy when purchased live. True easterners will tell you that there is only one way to thoroughly enjoy them: like lobster, plopped live into a kettle of boiling, salted water, and served whole with lots of melted butter on the side. Done this way, a mess of hard-shell Blue Crabs, usually weighing 1/4 lb to 1 lb each, will turn bright red and be cooked to perfection in approximately twenty minutes.

The larger Dungeness Crab of the Pacific, generally weighing between 1 3/4 lb and 4 lbs, will require a little longer time in the pot — twenty-five to thirty minutes, maximum.

How to Clean Soft-Shell Crabs

Most fish dealers will clean the soft-shell crabs for you when you are buying them fresh. However, since killing and cleaning them is easy and, in terms of freshness brings them that much sooner to your pan, here is a simple way for doing it yourself:

With a sharp knife or pair of scissors, cut off the face (the eyes and mouth parts) in a straight line, just behind the eyes.

Bend back the apron that folds under the body at the rear until it snaps. If properly done, this action will allow you to pull away the apron as well as the intestinal vein attached to it.

Lift each point at the sides of the crab's top shell and scrape away the gills — the gray-white feathery material.

Remove the stomach and drain it of all fluids by twisting the slit made to cut off the face.

Rinse the crab in cold, salted water. Pat dry with paper toweling. It is now ready for the pan.

While the taste of frozen soft-shell crabs is not nearly as perfect as that of fresh ones, consider that they already have been cleaned and need only be thawed before frying and grilling. Besides, they do offer the advantage of a soft-shell season, well beyond Mother Nature's run.

How to Store Soft-Shell Crabs

Having cleaned your catch or purchase, freezing soft shell crabs for a rainy or, better still, for a snowy day, is a simple task:

With the legs folded under the body, cover each crab with plastic wrap.

Place them in your freezer, spread in a single layer on a cookie sheet.

After they are frozen solidly, put each one in a freezer bag, seal, and return to the big, deep chill. Stored this way, your soft-shell crabs will keep up to six months.

How to Clean and Preserve Crab Shells

Having purchased live crabs or, if you are lucky enough to have picked up some on a beach during your own crabbing, you will want to keep the shells as unique and attractive serving cups for restuffing.

To re-use, scrub them well under cold, running water. Soak overnight in a solution of half a cup of baking soda added to one gallon of water. Rinse well on the following day, then boil in a pot of water laced with fresh baking soda. Rinse again and dry thoroughly for storing.

Looked after this way, the shells should hold up for awhile, at least until you replace them the next time you treat yourself to live crabs. A light spray of vegetable oil is recommended before each use.

How to Cook Soft-Shell Crabs

Every soft-shell crab purist has a favorite way to prepare them. However, the following methods are quick, easy, tried and true.

Sautéing
Dust the crabs with flour, then sauté in butter or vegetable oil over moderate heat until golden brown. Add lemon juice to the butter in the pan and, after moving the crabs to a platter, pour the mixture over them before serving.

Baking
Preheat oven to 400°F. Place the crabs, each one topped with a dab of butter, on a greased baking pan. Bake for about eight minutes on the mid-level rack of your oven.

Favorite Recipes

Stuffed Crabs
Serves 8

8   large female crabs
water for boiling 2 tbsp salt

Stuffing
1/4 cup	olive oil
1	clove garlic, peeled and finely chopped
1	small onion, finely chopped
3/4 lb	tomatoes, peeled, seeded and chopped
1 1/2 tbsp	parsley, finely chopped
1 tsp	cayenne pepper
11/2 tbsp	capers salt to taste

Topping
6 tbsp	dry bread crumbs
3 tbsp	olive oil

Drop the crabs into a large pot of salted, boiling water, cover. When the water has returned to the boil, cook for about three minutes. Remove the crabs and allow to drain. When they are cool enough to handle, remove the breastplate and pry off the back shell, keeping it intact.

Remove the meat from all the shells, cutting away any fat and eggs left on the crabs. Set aside.

Scrub six of the shells under cold, running water, scraping off any remaining debris. Dry and reserve.

To make the stuffing, heat the oil in a sauce pan and sauté garlic and onion until translucent and golden brown.

Add the tomatoes and all the other ingredients except the crab meat. Cook the mixture over medium-high heat until it is almost dry — about five to eight minutes. Stir in the crab meat and season with salt. Remove from heat

Stuff the reserved shells with the mixture Sprinkle with the bread crumbs and drizzle olive oil on top.

Just before serving, brown the stuffed crabs under the broiler until the tops are golden brown.

Recommended Wines

European

White Burgundy
Chardonnay
Sancerre
Soave
Pouilly-Fumé
Orvieto Riesling (dry)

North American

Chardonnay
Riesling (dry)
Sauvignon Blanc
Seyval Blanc
Fumé Blanc
Vidal (dry)

Recipes

Fried Crabs
Serves 4 – 6

12	soft-shell crabs
2	eggs, beaten
1/4 cup	milk
1 tsp	salt
3/4 cup	flour
3/4 cup	dry bread crumbs
	oil for frying

Clean the crabs, rinse and pat dry. In a mixing bowl, combine eggs, milk and salt. Combine flour and crumbs on a platter or bread board.

To bread the crabs, first dip them, one at a time, into the egg mixture, then roll them in the flour and crumbs.

For deep frying, preheat oil to 375°F. Put the crabs in the pan and fry for three or four minutes until golden brown. Drain on paper towels before serving.

To pan fry, place the breaded crabs in a heavy frying pan containing 1/4 inch of hot but not smoking oil. Fry until golden brown — about four minutes per side.

Favorite

Old-Fashioned Crab Cakes
Serves 4

Crab cakes are prominently featured on most Maryland restaurant breakfast menus as the specialty of the house.

To bring back the memory of a happy motor trip through the state, this recipe is worth trying:

1 lb	crab meat
1/2 cup	mayonnaise
3 tbsp	green peppers, chopped
2 tbsp	onion, finely chopped
2	eggs
2 tsp	Worcestershire sauce
1 tsp	dry mustard
	salt and pepper to taste
3/4 cup	dry bread crumbs
Garnish	chopped parsley and lemon wedges

In a mixing bowl, combine the crab meat, mayonnaise, green peppers, onion, Worcestershire sauce, mustard, salt and pepper. Shape into small patties and coat with bread crumbs.

Fry in a lightly oiled skillet for a few on each side, until golden brown.

Garnish with parsley and lemon wedges.

About Shrimp

Be Glad You're Not a Shrimp

When nude the shrimp tends to perplex
Because you cannot tell its sex
Which end is which, no one can say
For shrimps are inclined that way.
They have no bottom and no top
They simply start and then they stop.
Their love life must be very blah
Because Pa looks so much like Ma.

– From Shrimply Delicious *by Eva Jean Schulz*

Soft music, candlelight and a loved one by your side are the ground rules for the perfect dinner that includes a dish of shrimps. There is something rather sensuous about seeing the object of your desire dip one of these creatures in herb butter or a nippy cocktail sauce. Just as you always remember your first kiss, the day you ate your first great shrimp will remain unforgettable.

"It happened to us in Florida," a friend wrote. "We were driving along the coastal highway, north of Boca Raton, when we saw a simple little roadside restaurant. It had a miniscule sign but a huge parking lot. At the back was a wharf and, just as we arrived, a shrimp boat was chugging in to unload its catch. Half an hour later, a large bowl of deep-fried shrimps was set in the middle of our table. At first, we took our time peeling and dipping them in the house sauce, but soon found ourselves wolfing them down in vast quantities. Washed down with California Chablis poured from a big jug, they ruined us for almost any other shrimp."

Long, Long Ago ...

The ancient Romans ate shrimp as a starter before launching into serious drinking or love making. Marcus Apicius, one of their most famous epicures, even went to Africa — a long and dangerous voyage in those days — just to compare the local shrimp with those caught off the coast of his native Rome. A Portuguese explorer who travelled to West Africa discovered a river he named *Rio des Camaroes* or Shrimp River in a region we call the Camaroons. The Italian adventurer Giovanni Jacopo Casanova was convinced of the delicate shrimp's powers as a food of love. Even his aging companion Agnolo Torredane attributed his potency and long life to a diet of paella, heavily laced with shrimp. In 1770, Captain Cook came across a kingdom in the South Pacific whose ruler, then a gentleman in his eighties, told him that it was his royal duty to make love to every virgin in the land. Boasting that he had never slept twice with the same woman and could perform the sex act up to ten times a day, he attributed his remarkable libido to a steady in-take of shrimp.

A Confusing Creature

No one is quite sure what the shrimp's sex really is at any given time nor whether the plural of the word is shrimp or shrimps. We know it is a decapod — a ten-legged creature; however, almost any crustacean with ten legs that isn't a lobster or a crawfish, is called a shrimp. This gets even more confusing because of the prawn. (To clear up the mystery, see "Prawns and Scampi").

Around the world, shrimp can live on the muddy bottoms of deep or shallow waters, salt as well as fresh. In the northern hemisphere they are found off the coasts of Norway, Iceland, Greenland, and Alaska but there also are shrimp beds along the Atlantic and Pacific coasts of North, Central and South America. Each area has its own species — the most famous being the pink creatures that come from the Gulf of Mexico while the brown variety hails from Brazil.

Shrimps also are hermaphrodites, those creatures of mythology that unite both sexes under one carapace — the bonelike substance that covers their backs. Some spend their first and second year as active males and, by a mysterious process, become female in the third. Their breeding season is in late autumn or early winter when the larvae leave the mature female's body to swim about freely. Three months later, they settle down on the ocean floor.

Harvesting Shrimp

Before refrigeration, shrimps were only known in areas close to the sea. In fact, in the early days of North American shrimping nobody bothered to preserve them. It was strictly a catch-and-eat crop — a treat few inland folk could enjoy. Then, some industrious and ingenious Chinese, who had settled in Louisiana during the nineteenth century, started to dry shrimps and sell them around the world.

To harvest shrimp from the ocean in earlier times, people used square nets held open by wooden (later, metal) bars. To gather up the catch, the shrimper would wade through the shallow water at low tide, allowing the net's lower end to scrape along the ocean floor.

The industry was mechanized in the nineteenth century when horses were used to pull large dragnets through the water. When the first offshore shrimp trawlers appeared in 1917, they could stay at sea for up to ten days and bring in larger quantities of shrimp at one time.

Today, harvesting is done from commercial trawlers equipped with cone-shaped nets which are dragged along the bottom to gather up the shrimp. Another method, known as the otter trawl and mostly seen in the Gulf of Mexico, uses a net whose upper edge is supported by glass or aluminium floats while its sides are attached to two vane-shaped boards. When the gear is towed along the bottom, the water opens the net's mouth; the size of shrimp caught in this manner depends on the density of the net's mesh.

As soon as the shrimps are hauled into the trawler, they are beheaded, washed and put on ice. For canning, the harvest is immediately taken to a processing plant, inspected and moved by conveyor belt to be sorted and peeled by hand. As grading varies from area to area, the following is a basic grouping for the different sizes:

Tiny	–	75	to	100	per pound	
Small	–	35	to	45	"	"
Medium	–	25	to	35	"	"
Large	–	20	to	25	"	"
Jumbo	–	15	to	20	"	"
Giant	–	10	to	12	"	"

The Gulf of Mexico is still the world's richest shrimping ground which explains why the people who live in the region are the most demanding shrimp eaters. In New Orleans, for example, they insist on the whole animal rather than just the tail. Tomalley — the liver found in the head — is considered a great delicacy there.

How to Buy and Store Shrimp

Shrimp should be eaten fresh and handled carefully, even when frozen. Raw, they are called "green" and, as the name implies, should be greenish-grey or pinkish tan in color. When they are fresh they smell sweet. Look for the same quality in those that are frozen and/or thawed. A slight ammonia or medicinal odor indicates that deterioration has set in. Discard those that show black zones around the edges of their shells.

After shelling and deveining, two pounds of shrimp produce one pound of meat. To serve one person, you will need about one cup of cooked (shelled and deveined) shrimp — 3/4 lb raw or 7 oz frozen (shelled and deveined).

Canned shrimp cost about the same as those you can get at the fish market; when you buy them raw there is 47 per cent more waste but they are less expensive than cooked and prepared shrimp.

You can store raw shrimp for four to five days in the freezer compartment of your refrigerator; in a deep freeze they will retain their flavor for up to six months.

How to Clean Shrimp

If you have bought shrimps with their heads on, just twist them off and you will be left with the main part of the body which is the edible tail.

To shell, grasp each shrimp with one hand, slip your thumb under the shell at the wide end, behind the forward legs, and lift off. Moving forward, tear off two or three segments at a time. The intestinal canal, called vein or sand vein, running along the base of a groove in the animal's back, is generally removed if only for appearance's sake. Slit the shrimp down the back, lift out the vein or scrape it with a toothpick or the tip of a sharp knife.

Leave the tail intact for fried or cocktail dishes.

To remove the fishy odor and firm up the meat, follow this tip from an Asian chef:

Shell and devein shrimps in the usual way then soak for five minutes in a mixture of one tablespoon borax and two cups cold water. Rinse carefully under cold, running water until the shrimps are no longer slippery to the touch. Squeeze dry in paper toweling with your fingers.

How to Cook Shrimp

Cooking Times in Minutes		
	Shrimp	**Rock Shrimp**
Stewing	1 – 3	1 – 2
Baking	10	5 – 8
Sautéing	3 – 4	2 – 3
Broiling	2 – 3	2 – 3
Poaching	1 – 3	1 – 2
Stir Frying	2 – 3	1 – 2
Deep Frying	1 – 2	1 – 2

Poached Shrimp

Asian cuisine has a particularly felicitous way with shrimps that allows you to cook them without flavor loss.

Preferably, buy white shrimps as they have a gentler taste than the pink or red ones. Leave the shells on as this will preserve the flavor and prevent curling. If you are using frozen shrimps, do not defrost beforehand.

Add the shrimps to a pot of boiling water. After it has returned to the boil, cook no longer than three or four minutes. Drain immediately. Reserve the liquid for seasoning or use as a soup base.

From *Vietnamese Cookery* by Jill Nhu Huong Miller

About Shrimp

Recipes

Cioppino
Tadich Grill, San Francisco

Cooking Time: 2 1/2 hours Serves 4

Sauce

2 oz	olive oil
2 oz	butter
1/2	medium onion, chopped
1/2	celery stalk, chopped
1	medium carrot, chopped
1 tbsp	chopped fennel
1/2	medium bell pepper, chopped
1/2	leek stalk, white part only, chopped
1	28-oz can tomatoes, crushed
1 tbsp	tomato paste
3 1/2 cups	water
1 tbsp	salt
1/4 tsp	pepper
1/2 tsp	oregano
1/2 tsp	basil
1/4 tsp	thyme
4	bay leaves
dash	of cayenne pepper

Seafood

2 oz	olive oil
2 oz	butter

Chef John Canepa, the creator of this dish, kindly revealed to us five secrets for a cioppino delizioso:

1. *The fish must be absolutely fresh.*
2. *To enhance rather than mask the taste of the fish, the sauce with its wonderful herb aroma should be light — not strong and overbearing.*
3. *Make sure the fat in the skillet is hot. Sauté the fish before adding wine and sauce.*
4. *It is very important to reduce the wine during the sauté as evaporation removes the alcohol, leaving behind the wine's bouquet.*
5. *Do not cook the seafood in the sauce for hours as this toughens shrimps, clams, and scallops and makes the fish fall apart and become mushy. When served to your guests the fish should look and taste firm.*

1 tsp	garlic, finely chopped
2 tbsp	flour
8 oz	halibut, cut into 1/2 in x 2 in pieces
8 oz	swordfish, cut into 1/2 in x 2 in pieces
8	large scallops
8	large shrimps, shelled and deveined
4 oz	Bay shrimps
6 oz	crab meat
8 oz	dry white wine

Garnish 8 Cherrystone clams
1 tbsp parsley

To make the sauce, heat olive oil and butter in a heavy saucepan. Add onions and sauté over medium heat for about one minute. Do not brown. Add celery, carrots, fennel, bell pepper and leek. Braise for about five minutes. Add tomatoes, tomato paste, water, salt, pepper and remaining herbs and spices. Simmer sauce for at least two hours, keeping it consistently hot and stirred.

In a large frying pan, heat oil and butter. Add garlic and sauté for a few seconds. Lightly dust the seafood with flour. Add to the pan and sauté until golden — for about two minutes. Add the wine and stir for about one minute to reduce. Transfer sauce to the frying pan, cover and simmer for a further seven minutes.

Wash the clams carefully to remove the sand. Steam for approximately five minutes or until opened, or boil in a mixture of 1 cup water, 1/2 cup wine and 1 tbsp chopped onion.

Serve cioppino in an oval casserole or in a large soup dish, garnished with the clams and sprinkled with parsley.

Serve with toasted French bread, spread with butter, garlic, and oregano.

About Shrimp

Favorite Recipes

Stir-Fried Shrimp
Serves 4

2 lbs	shrimp
4 cups	water
1 tsp	salt
1	egg white
1 tsp	corn-flour
1 tbsp	oil

Shell, wash and devein the shrimps. Soak for thirty minutes in water to which 1/2 tsp salt has been added. Rinse and let drain for ten minutes. Pat dry.

Place shrimps in a bowl. Mix in egg white, corn-flour and salt. Cover and refrigerate for at least three hours — the longer the better.

Heat wok and add oil. When hot but not smoking, add half the mixture and stir with chop sticks. Cook no longer than 20 – 30 seconds. Drain well. Repeat for second batch.

Either serve immediately or store covered in the refrigerator to be reheated later.

From *Chinese Gastronomy* by Hsian Ju Lin and Tsuifeng Lin

Shrimp Steamed in Beer
Filet of Sole Restaurant, Toronto
Appetizer for 4

4 oz	butter
2	cloves garlic, chopped
1	celery stalk, diced
10 oz	beer
2 lb (16 – 20)	white shrimps, shell on
	salt and pepper to taste

Melt butter in a saucepan and add garlic and celery. Sauté for a few minutes.

Add beer and shrimps. Season with salt and pepper. Cover and steam for about five minutes or until the shrimp's color changes to orange-red. Do not overcook.

Ladle the shrimp, together with the liquid, into soup bowls. Shell and eat.

To mop up the delicious cooking liquid, serve with chunks of French bread.

Recommended Wines

European

White Burgundy
Chardonnay
Sancerre Soave
Pouilly-Fumé
Orvieto
Riesling (dry)

North American

Chardonnay
Riesling (dry)
Sauvignon Blanc
Seyval Blanc
Fumé Blanc
Vidal (dry)

About Shrimp

Prawns and Scampi

"Our shrimp have most prawny proportions."

Daily Telegraph, *London, 1865*

Nothing impresses a true shellfish gourmand more than meeting someone who actually knows the difference between a shrimp, a scampi and a prawn. Confusing these three can be expensive — there is a much higher premium on prawns, for instance, than on large shrimp. You've got to know your prawns and your scampi. Restaurants in many countries are not above fobbing off giant shrimps as prawns and sticking a higher price tag on them. There's even more confusion about a crustacean the Peruvians call *camaron* which is Spanish for shrimp. Although it has lobster-like claws, which shrimp do not have, it is more than likely a crawfish.

The Prawn

No one knows where the word "prawn" comes from. The Oxford English Dictionary defines it this way: "A small, long-tailed decapod marine crustacean ... larger than a shrimp, common to the coasts of Great Britain, and used as food."

Yet, in 1620, shrimps and prawns were considered as one and the same thing. About two hundred years later, however, the English began to distinguish them by size. Waverly Root, in his wonderful book *Food*, says that prawns "once confused an English court called upon to decide if it constitutes cruelty to these crustaceans to fry them to death instead of boiling them to death."

We always think of prawns as "the things with eyes." When they stare at you from your plate for the very first time, it can be a rather disconcerting experience. Unlike their generally accepted image, they are not necessarily larger than shrimp but slimmer with longer legs; when cooked, they also have a subtly different flavor.

Prawns have one thing in common with salmon. They, too, are anadromous — a marvelous word for describing animals that spend one part of their lives in fresh water and the other in the sea. Born in muddy shoals, they move to deeper waters when partially developed and migrate toward the ocean once they have reached maturity; at the end of four months, they move back to the warmer fresh-water spawning grounds.

Prawns also have most peculiar sex lives. They are male during their second and third years, switching to female in years three and four when eggs can be found on them between October and March.

Although prawns usually grow in the wild, in the past few years shellfish breeders in the southern United States began to stock ponds with a variety imported from Malaysia. Now cultivated in South Carolina and in Hawaii, these large, shrimp-like fresh-water animals are harvested in the autumn. They have a meaty tail, similar to that of the shrimp, but its flavor is slightly sweeter.

In Portugal and Spain, the common prawn is called *gamba*; in Portugal you may also meet *gamba rosada* which is a *carabinero* in Spain or the dark-red *gamba verhelho* which the Spanish view with almost cultist fervor and dish up as *langostino moruno*.

Simply boiled, the smaller ones are considered the best. They are then cooled and served in their shells — always with their heads on. The juice bursting from the head is ambrosia to langostino fetishists who insist that their best and most famous growing places are in the southern Spanish province of Andalusia — just where the Guadalquivir River flows into the Atlantic or, along the River Ebro, in the northern province of Asturias.

Eighty-five species of prawns and shrimps exist off Canada's west coast alone.

Prawns and Scampi

Six of them are commercially important, the Spot Prawn and the Side Stripe Shrimp having the highest value. Spot Prawns derive their name from the distinctive white spots on the first and fifth segments of their bodies. They grow to about 10 in (25 cm) in length and generally are harvested with traps on the rocky bottoms of the oceans — from Unalaska in the eastern Aleutians to Southern California, and from the Sea of Japan to the Korea Strait. The Side Stripe Shrimp reaches 8 in (20 cm) in length — second only to the prawn. It has long antennules but it is the striped abdomen that distinguishes it from all the others.

The Scampi

Scampi — the Italian plural of the word — is the other crustacean often referred to as a shrimp. This error is especially common in Italy where unscrupulous restaurateurs sometimes profit from the reputation of the prestigious Venetian Scampi. This delicacy is also known as the Norway Lobster — the smaller version of the Spiny Lobster. It is the same as the Dublin Bay Prawns, called that because Irish fishermen were the first to recognize their value; others simply threw them back because they did not think anybody would buy them. When Dublin street vendors, such as Molly Malone, started hawking them, they were named after the city and the bay on which it lies.

How to Buy and Prepare Prawns and Scampi

Prawns and scampi are greenish in color, firm to the touch, and should not smell of ammonia which would indicate the onset of deterioration. Seldom available live, they usually are sold frozen, both raw and cooked.

Plan to serve each person with one-half to one-third of a pound of cooked prawns or scampi.

To butterfly them, twist off and discard the claws. Snip off the feelers with a pair of scissors. Twist apart the body and the tail. Discard the body.

Peel off all but the last section of the tail shell. Cut through the back of the tail, almost, but not quite to the end. To prepare it for stuffing and broiling spread the two halves apart and flatten slightly.

How to Cook Prawns and Scampi

Cooking Times

Stewing	1 – 3	minutes
Baking	10	minutes
Sautéing	1 – 3	minutes
Broiling	2 – 3	minutes
Poaching	1 – 3	minutes
Stir Frying	1 – 2	minutes
Deep Frying	1 – 2	minutes

Shellfish Butter

Crush prawn bodies and shells in a mortar, together with softened butter until the mixture has the consistency of a paste. Force the paste through a fine-meshed sieve with a spatula. Discard the cartilage and shells remaining in the sieve. Keep refrigerated until ready to use.

Favorite

Prawn Soup

Sooke Harbour House, Vancouver Island   *Courtesy: Chef Michael Stadtlander*

Serves 4

3 cups	fish stock
2	shallots, peeled and chopped
3/4 cup	white wine
1 tbsp	lemon juice
1 1/2 cups	whipping cream
2 tsp	Pernod
1/4 cup	chopped fennel
1/4 cup	chopped anise hyssop leaves
	freshly ground black pepper
Garnish	4 whole prawns, uncooked and shelled with heads on
	4 sprigs fennel
	whole anise hyssop leaves

In a large pot, combine fish stock, shallots, white wine, lemon juice and one cup whipping cream. Bring to a boil and simmer for approximately ten minutes.

Meanwhile, combine 1/2 cup whipping cream, Pernod, fennel, anise hyssop leaves and shelled prawns in a blender or food processor. Process until smooth.

Add the mixture to the stock and simmer just long enough to heat through.

Serve in large soup bowls, sprinkled with freshly ground black pepper and garnished with a whole prawn, a sprig of fennel and the anise hyssop leaves.

Prawns and Scampi

Poached Prawn or Scampi

As prawns usually are poached whole, the tails do not need deveining.

They are best cooked in a good *court bouillon* but should be left unshelled to enhance the stock. The poaching liquid can be salted water or water mixed with white wine, lemon juice or wine vinegar and flavored with onions or fresh herbs — parsley, dill, fennel.

All vegetable garnishes should be prepared and partially cooked in advance. To intensify the flavor of the broth, use only enough liquid to barely cover the shellfish and the ingredients in the pot. Keep the poaching liquid at a gentle simmer.

Once the prawns or scampi have been poached, they may be used for other dishes. If the recipe calls for them to be cut up or shelled, follow the instructions for butter flying.

Recommended Wines

European

White Burgundy
Chardonnay
Sancerre
Soave
Pouilly-Fumé
Orvieto Riesling (dry)

North American

Chardonnay
Riesling (dry)
Sauvignon Blanc
Seyval Blanc
Fumé Blanc
Vidal (dry)

Prawns and Scampi

Recipes

Prawns with Green Chinese Radish

Sooke Harbour House, Vancouver Island   Courtesy: Chef Michael Stadtlander

Serves 4

1/4 cup	olive oil
40	large shelled prawns, heads left on
3 cups	fish stock
1/2 cup	white wine
1/4 cup	rice vinegar
1 in	knob ginger, finely minced
2	cloves garlic
1 tsp	honey
1	large green Chinese radish (approx. weight 12 oz), peeled and sliced into 1/8 in thick slices
1	bunch green onions, white part only, cut into 2 in – 3 in lengths
1 lb	fresh linguine, cooked
Garnish	edible chrysanthemum petals

Heat olive oil in a frying pan over moderate heat.

Sauté prawns on both sides. Remove and keep warm.

To a large pot, add fish stock, wine, rice vinegar, ginger and garlic. Reduce and add honey.

Place linguine on a large plate. Arrange prawns on top. Heat vegetables in the glaze and place on top. Pour glaze over them and garnish the dish with chrysanthemum petals.

Favorite

Prawns and Scampi

The Strange Abalone

Oh! Some folks boast of quail on toast,
Because they think it's tony;
But I'm content to owe my rent
And live on abalone.

– George Sterling

Abalones are among the most mysterious of all the sea animals. The Maoris of New Zealand believed them to be the offspring of the guardians of the ocean, traveling from coast to coast as messengers of love. The vast number of abalone shells found in Maori middens attest to their wide use, not only as a food. They polished the shells to represent the eyes in their carvings and shaped them into such implements as fishhooks and reflecting lures. The abalone therefore, became one of the earliest creatures humans used for catching fish. The Indians of the Pacific Northwest made ornaments from the shells and, since they also used them as currency, they were considered a source of wealth, even by those living inland.

The reason why these shellfish were so valuable and so savagely exploited everywhere, was the magnificent nacre (mother-of-pearl) of their inner shells, lavish with opalescent blues, iridescent pinks and deep purples. These shells were used, for thousands of years, in jewelry, as inlays for furniture and in such highly prized artifacts as boxes and bowls. More recently, curios that contain these increasingly rare shells, make that part of the abalone almost twice as valuable as its flesh.

In the 1870s, large numbers of Chinese and Japanese men came to North America to work on the railroads. When they landed on the California coast, they were surprised to find that they could scoop abalone out of the sea by the basketful at low tide. Back home, where it had been considered a great delicacy, it was almost extinct because it had been over-fished for so many years.

A new industry was born when these men began to send shiploads of these fragile beauties to China and Japan. Alas, the once-bountiful California shores were soon as bereft of abalone as the older Asian ranges. They now are found mainly off the California shores and in smaller grounds off the coast of Mexico. Today, divers must harvest them from deeper and deeper waters. A closed season has been declared with limits on the size — 7 in (18 cm) — and the numbers which can be taken. It also is against the law to even send abalone out of the State of California. Recent cultivation attempts there and in Japan have been only mildly successful so far, since the science is still very much in its infancy.

The abalone is a marine gastropod that looks like a large, single-shelled clam with the open side glued to a rock. It is really a flat sea snail. It derives its name "ear form" from the shape of its shell. The few whorls increase in diameter so that the widest part is the last whorl.

The abalone is a slow-growing creature; it takes the female six years to spawn. The number of eggs she produces depends on her size: if she grows to about 4 in (10 cm) in diameter, she can produce 100,000 eggs; measuring 10 in to 12 in (25 to 30 cm) in diameter, she can produce two million. The breeding season is between February and April 1. After ova and sperm have been released into the ocean, the male and female wait for a chance encounter of the closest kind.

Apart from its Latin name, *haliotus tuberculata*, the abalone is known as sea snail, Venus' Ear, ear-shell, and Linnaeus (after the Swedish botanist Carolus Linnaeus). The Portuguese call it *orelha*, the Spanish, *oreja de mar*, and the French refer to it as *ormeau, ormier, six-yeux*, or *oreille de mer*. It is called *ormer* in the Channel Islands where, at one time, there was almost a cult surrounding these animals. As Waverly Root tells us in his book *Food*, four times during the winter, when the "ormering tide" uncovers the Jersey and Guernsey shores, everything was closed down to give the population time to swarm over the rocks to pry loose the exposed ormers. Much to the chagrin of the natives, who had taken dozens and dozens over the years, the practice was banned in 1972 to save the species from extinction.

One hundred species exist in the world, eight of them along the Pacific coast of North America. The Red Abalone *(haliotus rufescens)* is found in California, from north of San Francisco to the southern tip of the State, with the biggest concentration around Monterey. It can weigh up to 8 lbs (3.5 kg), the average being about half that much. We also know of a small, pink abalone with a wavy pink shell which is very gregarious and tends to gather in groups. The tiny ones, which live off the Florida Keys, have no commercial value because of their size and are found only in waters up to 600 feet (182 meters) deep. There also is a Green, a Black, a White, a Pinto and a Northern Abalone.

The Awabi is commercially cultivated in Japan where thousands of. metric tons are taken each year. Displayed in a shell, not necessarily the one it was born with, it is about 1 in (2.5 cm) thick and the size of a hand; its colors range from pale peach to gray or even blue. Other species occur along the coasts of Asia and Africa, in the Mediterranean, and in grounds stretching from the Channel Islands down to and along the west coast of France.

The appearance of the shell is indicative of the species. Although protecting the body, it permits the abalone's muscular foot to move along the ocean bottom or cling to hard surfaces with tremendous tenacity. If the animal is startled by an enemy, it clamps its huge foot so firmly to the rock that it is almost impossible to pry loose.

Along the edge of the shell are a number of breathing holes. As it grows, new holes appear and those not in use seal over. The gills are under the holes. Once the foot is attached to a rock, the gills take in oxygen by pumping water into the shell and then discharging it through the holes.

The abalone is a strict vegetarian that feeds on seaweed, using its tiny rasp-like teeth. Because it's not a filter feeder, it is immune to red tides and does not even build up bacteria in heavily polluted waters.

Like other univalves, its flesh has about the same texture as rubber. However, when the delicate white steaks have been tenderized and properly prepared, they become soft as butter. They have a distinctively sweet and succulent flavor.

Canned abalone, either minced or in cubes, comes from Japan where the largest quantities of this shellfish are consumed. The Japanese also make it into a dried product by reducing it to ten per cent of its original weight, and sell it shredded as *kaiho* or powdered as *meiho* ...

How to Catch Abalone in the Wild

Look under rock ledges as the abalone tends to shun the light. Once you have spied one, move quickly so that it cannot attach itself more firmly to the rock. Pry it loose with a flattened bar or let the animal seize hold of a board laid beside it.

How to Prepare Abalone

The mushroom-shaped piece of meat has a stem by which the muscle is attached to the shell. The cap section consists of the foot that includes the solid flesh, the mouth and an intestinal vein covered with tough skin.

With an abalone shucker — a short-handled, spatula-like instrument — pry away the flesh from the shell. Free the flesh by severing the stem-like muscle with a sharp knife. Cut away and discard the viscera, the dark skin around the edges and across the surface, as well as the mouth and the large green gut.

Cut the tough meat into strips and tenderize it by pounding with a wooden mallet.

How to Cook Abalone

Be sure to tenderize the abalone steaks before sautéing, broiling or stir frying. All seafood, but especially mollusks, toughen when over-cooked. To return them to their delicate state, you must stew them for at least fifteen minutes.

Cooking Times

Sautéing	no longer than 45 seconds on each side
Broiling	2 minutes
Stir Frying	2 minutes
Deep Frying	2 minutes

Abalone Steaks

Slice the foot into steaks, each 3/8 in (1 cm) thick. With a wooden mallet, a rolling pin or a hammer, gently pound the meat for about three minutes. Be sure not to over-tenderize the steaks as they can become mushy. To improve texture and flavor, store in the refrigerator for one or two days.

Sauté, broil, or deep fry the steaks, making sure not to overcook them.

Beer is an excellent accompaniment for this dish.

The Strange Abalone

Recipes

Abalone Chowder
Serves 4

Unless you are determined to use fresh abalone, those from a can are well suited for this recipe and available at Asian food markets.

2	cans abalone meat, or
6	steaks, pounded and cubed
4	bacon slices, diced
1	medium onion, finely chopped
1	small garlic clove, crushed
1	large potato, peeled and diced
1 1/2 cups	hot water
3 cups	milk
1 tbsp	butter
	salt and pepper to taste

In a heavy chowder kettle or Dutch oven, lightly brown the bacon. Set aside. Pour off all but two tablespoons of the fat. Add meat, onion and garlic to the pot. Sauté until golden brown.

Add hot water, potato and reserved bacon. Cover and simmer until tender.

In a saucepan, heat the milk with the butter; be sure not to let it boil. Add to the chowder and sprinkle with salt and pepper to taste. Remove from heat, stir and serve.

Sautéed Abalone with Hazelnut-Lime Butter Sauce

Sooke Harbour House, Vancouver Island   Courtesy: Chef Pia Carroll

4	abalone in the shell
2	shallots, chopped
1	clove garlic, chopped
1/4 cup	pure apple-cider vinegar
4 oz	fish stock
4 oz	white wine
1/2 cup	cold unsalted butter pats
juice	from 1/2 lime
1/3 cup	toasted hazelnuts, ground
1 oz	clarified butter

The abalone can be frozen first to tenderize the muscle. When thawed, remove from shell with a large spoon. Discard viscera. Wash abalone to remove the black coating. With a sharp knife, cut vertically into 1/8 in-wide slices — not steaks. Set aside.

To make the sauce, combine shallots, garlic, vinegar, fish stock and wine in a saucepan. Cook over high heat to reduce to half a cup. Strain and reserve.

Reduce heat to very low and whisk in butter pats, piece by piece. Add lime juice and hazel nuts and stir for a few seconds until blended.

Heat clarified butter in a sauté pan. Add the abalone and cook briefly on both sides — about fifteen seconds. Arrange the slices overlapping on a platter.

To serve, spoon the sauce onto heated plates.

Recipes

Abalone Fritters
Serves 4

1	large or 2 small abalones
1/2 cup	flour
1 cup	milk
2	eggs, beaten
1 1/2 tsps	baking powder
1 1/2 tsps	salt
	oil for deep frying
Garnish	chopped parsley
	lemon wedges

Put the meat through the fine blade of a food chopper or cut into small pieces and chop in a food processor with 3 or 4 on/off pulses. Transfer to a large bowl.

Add flour, milk, eggs, baking powder and salt. Mix well. Heat oil to 375°F. Drop the batter into the hot fat, a few spoons full at a time. Fry until golden brown.

Sprinkle the fritters with parsley and garnish with the lemon wedges.

Recommended Wines

European

White Burgundy
Verdicchio
White Bordeaux
Mueller-Thurgau
Pinot Grigio
Sylvaner

North American

Chablis
Riesling (dry)
Sauvignon Blanc
Seyval Blanc
Gewuerztraminer (dry)
Vidal

The Beloved Conch

*"It's no longer clear who first earned the nickname "conch,"
whether it was the Tory sympathizers who went to the Bahamas
to escape the American Revolution – "We would rather eat conch
than go to war" – or the English who came to Key West
in the 1880s from the Bahamas."*

— *J. McClane* The Encyclopedia of Fish Cookery

Passionate eaters of conch know that the word is pronounced Conk, as in a blow to the head. Its long and honorable history began in October, 1492 when Christopher Columbus landed on San Salvador, the eastern most of the Bahama Islands. The region was populated by the Arawak Indians, a kind, gentle and creative people who thrived on the meat of the conch and made all manner of artefacts — chisels, ax blades, trumpets and ceremonial carvings — from its lovely shell.

These islands were colonized by Europeans and the conch became an important part of their daily lives. When some of them eventually left and moved to the Florida Keys, they brought it with them as a staple of their diets. In fact, these early pioneers, who knew how to make things from the flotsam of the sea, became so closely identified with it that the charming dwellings they created in Key West soon were known as "conch houses." Today, they are at a premium far beyond anything these settlers could have dreamed possible. Anyone born in that part of Florida still is known as a Conch. The term was originally an insult when used by outsiders but, perversely, is considered as a compliment by the natives.

The conch also goes by such names as whelk, scungilli, and sea snail. In fact, whelk and conch sometimes are used interchangeably even though they belong to different biological families and come from different geographic locations. The whelk prefers the cooler, more northerly waters, whereas the conch prefers the warm waters of the south.

The whelk is a carnivore that can be caught by "trotting" — casting lines baited with live crabs. Its meat is darker than that of the conch and has a stronger flavor. The outside of its thick-walled, spiral-shaped shell, which can grow to 9 in (22.5 cm) in diameter, is dull white, tan or yellowish gray, while the inside is typically yellow.

Conchs, on the other hand, have shells with a lusciously pink interior. Their meat is light and sweet and tastes very much like a mild clam, only more exotic. In North America, they now are abundant only around the Florida Keys. Their season is from spring to fall when they can be bought live or cooked, either whole or minced.

The Horse Conch of Florida, the largest of the univalves, can grow up to two feet (61 cm) in diameter, but the most magnificent of all is the 10 in Queen Conch (*strombus gigas*) which can only be found in the Keys. Its shell, pale tan on the outside and looking almost like porcelain on the inside, ranges in color from bright pink to flaming orange-red.

Although gourmands like to make a distinction between the "thin-lipped" edible Pink or Queen Conch and the "thick-lipped" Samba that inhabit the same areas of Florida and the Bahamas, most experts believe they are one and the same animal, just different in age. The bright blue shell with pinkish interior belongs to the older Samba, recognizable by its very thick lip, whereas the younger specimen has a pink lip that is, naturally, much thinner.

The conch is a herbivore that favors the sandy ocean shores. Because of its narrow foot, it cannot shuffle along like other gastropods. The conch sticks its foot into the sand and pushes itself forward with every move, leaping about half the length of its shell. To keep the outside world at bay, its strong operculum — the horny plate that covers the opening of the shell — allows it to withdraw into its own quiet world — the one we try to listen to when we hold a conch shell to our ears and imagine we hear the murmur of the sea.

How to Preserve Conch Shells

If you are in the Florida Keys and lucky enough to find a live conch, you surely will want to keep its beautiful shell.

To clean, immerse it in boiling water for five to ten minutes. Let the water cool down slowly. Remove the shell and wash it with soap and water. Let it dry before applying a light film of good olive oil which will make it shiny and enhance its beauty even more.

How to Buy and Prepare Conch

A word of warning: wherever conch is available, check with the local authorities to make sure it is safe to eat as the meat of some has been known to cause vomiting. Boiling it until the water froths, pouring off the liquid and cooking it a second time in fresh water, is a method that sometimes works to counteract this emetic effect.

To test whether a conch is alive, touch the movable disk (operculum) at its shell opening; it will retract if it is alive. Hidden inside the shell are the organs and an elongated mass of flesh. Covered by a tough skin, they are attached by a muscle to the spiked top of the shell.

To extract the flesh, hold the conch crown side up. Knock a hole into the shell with a hammer, 1 in (2.5 cm) below the top, making it large enough to get inside with the tip of a small knife.

To sever the muscle, insert the blade into the hole and move it back and forth. Then pull the flesh through the operculum that protrudes from the mouth of the

Recipes

shell until it is freed. Using a sharp knife, start at the crown end to cut away the soft stuff — the viscera and the eyes. Discard.

Find the intestinal vein that runs down the length of the body. Cut it out and discard. Under cold running water, rinse the channel from which the vein was removed. Peel off and discard the skin and cut away the operculum plus any remaining tough bits of orange membrane.

Despite the fact that the conch only feeds on plants, its meat is tough and must be tenderized like that of the abalone. Place the shucked conch in a bowl. Cover with fresh lime juice and allow to marinate at room temperature for about two hours. Drain and pat dry. Using a wooden mallet, pound each piece for two to three minutes or until the firm flesh becomes flexible and soft but not mushy. As an alternative, you may wish to put the flesh through a meat grinder or food processor.

How to Cook Conch

In Bahamian and Florida Keys kitchens, the use of spices is a fiery-hot subject. However, only individual tastes and preferences can determine how much Tabasco, bird peppers and hot pepper sauce should be added to various conch dishes. In the South, the rule of thumb is, of course, that hotter is better. We agree.

Cooking Times		
Stewing	1 1/2 – 3	hours
Sautéing	3 – 5	minutes
Stir Frying	2 – 3	minutes
Deep Frying	2	minutes

Conch Chowder
Serves 4

1/4 lb	salt pork, diced
1	medium Bermuda onion, finely chopped
4 cups	water
2 1/2 cups	tomatoes, fresh or canned
4 tbsp	tomato paste
3	medium potatoes, diced
1	Key lime, seeded and finely chopped
2	bay leaves
juice	of 1 Key lime
1	whole bird pepper or a few drops of Tabasco (optional)
3	conchs, cleaned, tenderized and finely diced

In a large kettle or Dutch oven, brown salt pork. Add the onion and cook until transparent.

Add remaining ingredients and bring to a simmer.

Add conch meat and cook over low heat for two hours or until tender. Serve hot.

Recipes

Conch Stew
Serves 4

	Meat from 6 conchs
3 cups	water, fish stock, wine or a combination thereof
1	medium onion, chopped
3	carrots, scraped and diced
1	stalk celery, chopped
4	tomatoes, quartered (optional)
1/4 lb	salt pork
3	scallions, chopped
1	clove garlic, crushed
1 tbsp	olive oil
1/2 tsp	ground cinnamon
	salt and pepper to taste
	bouquet garni-parsley sprigs, celery leaves, bay leaf, dried, hot chili pepper
juice	from 1 fresh lime
Garnish	diced red and green pepper, lightly sautéed

Cube the meat and cover with the liquid of your choice. Simmer in a large pot for one hour.

Remove the lid and allow the stew to cook over low heat for half an hour longer or until the liquid is reduced by one quarter.

Heat the olive oil in a frying pan and sauté salt pork, scallions and garlic for five minutes. When the salt pork has browned and the scallions are transparent, season with cinnamon, salt and pepper. Add bouquet garni.

Add the seasoned salt pork to the stewing liquid and continue cooking for fifteen minutes or until the meat is tender. Discard bouquet garni and season to taste with lime juice.

Serve with rice garnished with red and green peppers.

Recommended Wines

European

White Burgundy
Verdicchio
White Bordeaux
Mueller-Thurgau
Pinot Grigio
Sylvaner

North American

Chablis
Riesling (dry)
Sauvignon Blanc
Seyval Blanc
Gewuerztraminer (dry)
Vidal

The Beloved Conch

Conch Salad
Serves 4

	Meat from 1 conch
juice	of 1 fresh lime
1	small Bermuda onion, finely chopped or thinly sliced
1	small bell, hot jalapeno or Havana pepper, finely chopped
Garnish	lettuce leaves and chopped celery

Tenderize the meat and cut into 1/4 in cubes.

Add enough lime juice to cover.

Sprinkle with onion slices and chopped pepper. Let stand for fifteen minutes.

Toss the conch meat and the vegetables. Season to taste with salt and pepper. Marinate in the refrigerator for four to six hours, stirring frequently.

Line individual salad bowls with lettuce leaves. Add the salad. Garnish with celery and spoon some marinade over each serving.

As an alternative, marinate the chopped onion in lime juice for five minutes. Add to the conch meat and mix. Season with salt and pepper to taste.

Chill before serving.

The Magic Oyster

"A loaf of bread" the Walrus said,
"Is what we chiefly need:
Pepper and vinegar besides
Are very good indeed –
Now, if you're ready, Oyster dear,
We can begin to feed."

"O Oysters," said the Carpenter,
"You've had a pleasant run!
Shall we be trotting home again?"
But answer came there none –
And this was scarcely odd, because
They'd eaten everyone.

– From The Walrus and the Carpenter *by Lewis Carroll*

The Solitary Oyster safely dominates the list of such mysterious aphrodisiacs as ground reindeer antlers, garter belts and black silk stockings. It is said that the crafty Casanova devoured dozens of them before setting out to prove his masculinity. In writings about him, there are many learned and leering references that compare his fascination with oysters to his insatiable appetite for women. Don Juan and Henry VIII also adored oysters, and courtiers at the table of Louis XIV apparently watched in awe as their king devoured as many as one hundred in one single sitting. More recently, Tommy Greene of Maryland won a spot in the *Guinness Book of Records* for downing 288 — six pounds — of these succulent mollusks in just over ninety seconds!

In ancient times, the Roman Emperor Aulus Vitellius apparently could eat as many as one thousand at one time. To show how much the Romans thought of oysters, they even struck a coin — the denarius — in their honor, setting its value equal to that of a single oyster. It is said that the mountains of shells discovered among the ruins of Rome were proof that the Roman emperors quickly laid claim to all the oyster beds in the territories they conquered as these shells must have come from oysters harvested in the coastal waters of England, France and the outer reaches of their empire. The Romans' efforts to increase their supplies through aquaculture — the farming of oysters — is described in various writings, dating back to as early as the fourth century, B.C. Indeed, throughout history, oysters have been present on many occasions — from formal banquets where royalty sat down to dine to bacchanalian victory feasts given by generals who wanted to reward their weary warriors. In North America, the Indians, in addition to wild turkeys, brought oysters from nearby Plymouth Rock to the table of the Pilgrim Fathers when they prepared to celebrate their first Thanksgiving in the New World.

"Eat Fish Live Longer — Eat Oyster Love Longer"

These words on a sign advertising a once-famous, alas now gone, Toronto seafood restaurant lead us to ask ourselves whether there is any modern evidence of the aphrodisiac qualities ascribed to the oyster. An examination of its value as a food may provide us with a clue: the average market-sized oyster contains only sixty calories — less than 300 calories per pound of oyster meat; it is high in vitamins and minerals, rich in calcium, phosphorus, potassium, iodine, iron, copper and zinc; in fact, the experts tell us, oysters have twenty times more zinc than their combined copper-iron content.

According to these same experts, zinc is essential for the production of testosterone — the male sex hormone — which is responsible for the development and maintenance of masculine characteristics. Further medical studies have shown that zinc is the chief contributor to a healthy prostate gland.

The Oyster and its Shell

Whatever influence oysters may have on our sex lives, their own are strangely fascinating, to say the least. In fact, it is all but impossible to determine their gender, as most of them are born male, turn female when they are about four years old, then carry with them the organs of both sexes for the rest of their lives.

Some Welsh scientists discovered in 1973 that oysters even have moods. By monitoring their heartbeat, they found they grew plumper and faster when they were happy in their surroundings, but closed up tightly, which prevented them from breathing and feeding properly, when they were unhappy.

Oyster shells are rough, craggy and even look uninviting. Their colors vary and usually are a motley mix of various shades of brown, gray, green and white on the outside. Unlike the roughly symmetrical shells of other bivalves, the two halves differ in shape. The lower one, which cradles the oyster in its liquor or juice, is concave and cupped, while the flat, lid-like upper shell seals it shut. A large adductor muscle attached to both halves controls the opening and closing. Anyone who has attempted to open or "shuck" an oyster shell for the first time knows just how powerful it is.

Once opened, the inside of the shell is smooth to the touch and dull-white in color, except for the dark scar left by the adductor muscle when it is severed from the shell.

Oysters are motionless, except in the very early stages of their development. They spend their time attached to rocks on the warm floor of shallow bays into

The Magic Oyster

which rivers flow, or in estuaries where salty tides mix with fresh river water. It is here where they do what all bivalves do best — they pump water — fifty to one hundred pounds a day and, depending on their size, take on the taste of that water and its minerals as it passes through them.

When oyster aficionados boast about their favorites, they frequently cite the shell's size, shape and texture. However, it surely is the oyster's taste that has singled it out as one of the world's finest foods.

What Does an Oyster Taste Like

Salty? Buttery with a hint of copper? The answer is yes to both of the above.

Some say, the oyster's true delight is that it is so subtly flavored and, depending on the water from which it came, will taste substantially different, even if it hails from the same part of the country but from different beds within the same bay.

There are oysters aplenty for every taste and the true oyster lover will want to sample them all. The following is a listing of the more popular types favored by North Americans:

Malpeque
Comes from Malpeque Bay, Prince Edward Island. Its deeply cupped, long, slender, red-dish-brown shell holds a lot of juice. Considered by many to be the "gourmet" oyster.

Blue Point
This "oyster-bar oyster," which comes from Long Island Sound near Blue Point, N.Y., outsells all others, according to the people behind the counter at the renowned Oyster Bar at New York City's Grand Central Station. It also is much touted by chefs as the ideal cooking oyster.

Belon
Originally from the Belon River in Brittany, it is now grown in Nova Scotia and Maine. Although tough to open because of its flat, compact, rounded shell with fluted edges, its rapidly growing fan-club members say the treat inside is well worth the effort.

Wellfleet
Coming from Wellfleet Harbor on Cape Cod Bay, it has such a large and loyal following that the most fanatical oyster lovers will pass up others if Wellfleets are unavailable.

Olympia
These tiny nuggets — about the size of a quarter with meat the size of a dime — from Washington State are well worth a taste test. Regrettably, they are seldom served in restaurants, as they are not much fun to shuck.

Golden Frill
This west-coast beauty, easily recognized by its distinctive frilly-edged shell, continues to grow in popularity in the Vancouver area.

Contuit
Comes from Nantucket Sound and is in strong competition with the Wellfleet oyster.

Kent Island
This fat, saline treat from Chesapeake Bay is widely featured in east-coast shellfish bars.

Box Oyster
Coming from Gardiner's Bay off Long Island, it is so huge that you need a knife and fork to eat it.

Bras d' Or

Slightly smaller than a Malpeque and coming from Cape Breton Island's Bras d'Or Lakes, it is gaining popularity, thanks, in part, to aquaculture efforts. The constant salinity of these landlocked salt-water lakes gives it a distinctive flavor.

Waiter, There' s a Pearl in My Oyster!

The chances of finding a pearl in an American (Eastern, Atlantic) oyster are about as good as winning the lottery. Natural pearls come from the pearl oyster which is native to the warmer waters of the Pacific. Specially cultivated for jewelry, it takes up to three years to produce a pearl of marketable size, and the average yield is about twenty pearls for every 35,000 oysters.

Although North American oysters are not the pearl-bearing kind, they do produce pearls of a sort that are of little value except, perhaps, as a keepsake of a dinner at which you chipped a tooth.

The inner layer of the American oyster — a lining of calcium carbonate that reflects light — is called mother-of-pearl. It was valued by American Indians who strung its shells on thongs and used them as wampum or money.

William Butler's Warning

*"It is unseasonable and unwholesome in all months
that have not an R in their name to eat an oyster."*
— William Butler *Dyet's Dry Dinner (1599)*

While oysters can be eaten in months whose names do not contain the letter R, oyster lovers will tell you that they are at their succulent best in the months that do contain the R. A "bad" oyster eaten at any time of the year will make you seriously ill and, in the days before proper refrigeration, many probably spoiled in transit when shipped between May and August. Thanks to modem transportation, it now is possible to rush them to markets around the world in record time and enjoy them fresh all year round.

The real reason why oysters are less flavorful and tasty during those R-less months is that this happens to be their spawning period when they use their entire intake of food and nutrients to produce more oysters.

A word of warning to those who wish to gather oysters in the wild: always check with local or regional marine or fisheries authorities before taking any from oyster beds discovered during a seaside outing and while snorkeling or scuba diving. Make sure it is legal to take them and remember that oysters only are safe to eat if you know what they have been eating!

How to Buy and Store Oysters

When buying oysters in the shell, choose only those which are tightly closed. Reject any with partially gaping shells that do not shut quickly when handled, as well as those in cracked or broken shells.

Shucked oysters — sold by the pint or quart — should be plump, glistening and sweet smelling. Avoid those that contain more than ten per cent liquid by weight.

Wrapped in seaweed or in a damp towel, oysters can be stored in the refrigerator, but never longer than seven days. Oysters should never be frozen.

How to Shuck Oysters

To this day, no machine has been invented that could properly do the shucking job. Although you'll probably never match the 300-per-hour output of professional shuckers employed by packing plants, with a little practice, you should eventually manage to open two or three dozen in the same length of time.

With a stiff brush, scrub the oysters under cold, running water. Not to spoil their natural flavor, do not let them sit in water as they will only absorb it. Professional shuckers suggest that before opening an oyster, you "study" it to spot the point where the shell is most likely to give — usually at the hinge or on the rounded edge. They also think it's a good idea to shuck them over a strainer, to catch the bits of shell as well as the juice.

Wear a heavy glove (oven mitt) or wrap the oyster in a towel. Then grasp it firmly in your left hand (if you are right handed), with its cupped or heavy side down. Insert the tip of a sharp oyster knife between the two shells on the rounded side or at the hinge. Twist and wiggle the blade to force them apart. Once the bivalve has released its suction-like grip, sever the muscle by sliding the blade along the inside of the upper shell. Remove the shell, then carefully slide the knife under the oyster to cut through the lower muscle. For serving, meat and juice now should be on the curved "half shell."

Here are two other methods for getting under the shell:

1. Breaking in: with the deep shell down, hold the oyster firmly atop a block of wood, allowing the "bill" or edge of the shell to jut out just beyond the edge of the block.

   Using the tip of a small hammer or a pair of pliers, snap off the edge of the shell. Slide the oyster knife into the opening, working it back and forth until the adductor muscle is freed from the top shell. To sever the bottom muscle, dip the blade into the cradle shell below the meat. Be careful not to pierce the oyster when you use the knife as a lever to pry the shells apart.

   A word of warning: Always check the oyster in the half shell to see if it contains bits of shell which may have broken off during the "break in."

2. Baking in: scrub the shells with a stiff brush under cold, running water. To relax the adductor muscle and ease the task of opening the oysters, microwave on high, three or four at a time; for one minute. Serve as is or use in your favorite recipe.

How to Eat Oysters

Most North Americans prefer their oysters raw. What better way to start a meal than with a half or full dozen glistening in their shells, on a platter of crushed ice!

In a manner bordering on religious ritual, purists lift the oyster unadorned from the tray. They bring the side of the shell furthest from the hinge to their lips and then, usually with eyes closed, they dip the shell, ever so gently, allowing the oyster and its liquid to slide into their mouths.

When dining with a member of the opposite sex, it is becoming increasingly de rigueur to "toast" each other with the first oyster. In this ceremony, the lovers frequently take it from each other's tray and touch the edges of the shells across the table as they would glasses when drinking champagne.

Recipes

Grilled Oysters with Pear and Anise Hyssop Butter

Sooke Harbour House, Vancouver Island   *Courtesy: Chef Michael Stadtlander*

Appetizer for 4

1/4 cup	olive oil
1 dozen	oysters
5 ozs	pear cider
2	pears, peeled, cored and sliced
juice	of 1 lemon
1/4 cup	anise hyssop leaves, finely chopped
3 ozs	unsalted butter
Garnish	if available, 2 anise hyssop flowers, removed from stem

Brush broiler with olive oil and preheat until moderately hot. (Or heat olive oil in skillet to moderate heat.) Place oysters on broiler and grill on both sides. Remove and keep warm.

In a saucepan cook cider vinegar until reduced by half. Add the pears and poach until tender. Remove and set aside. Add lemon juice and anise hyssop leaves to the vinegar. Whisk in the butter over very low heat.

To serve, place the oysters on four small plates and pour sauce over each. Garnish with hyssop flowers.

Guinness and Oyster Soup

Courtesy: Chef Chris McNulty

Serves 4

1	onion, finely chopped
8	fresh oysters, shucked
1 tbsp	butter
1 tbsp	flour
1/2 bottle	Guinness beer
2 cups	fish stock
2 – 3 drops	oyster sauce
	salt and pepper to taste
1/2 tsp	sugar
2 tbsp	table cream

Garnish	finely chopped parsley
	4 whole oysters, shucked

In a large pot, sweat the onions in the butter until transparent but not colored. Add the oysters together with as much of their natural juices as possible. Cook two to three minutes. Add the flour and mix. Cook over low heat for one minute, stirring constantly.

Remove from the heat and whisk in the beer. Return to the heat and slowly stir in the fish stock. Bring to a boil, add the oyster sauce and simmer for five minutes.

Puree the soup in a blender or food processor. Return to a clean pot, season and add sugar. Bring to a boil. Add half the cream without re-boiling.

Ladle into four warmed soup bowls, adding the remaining cream to each. Garnish with parsley and one whole oyster per serving.

Note: Oyster sauce can be purchased at any Asian food store.

Recipes

Oysters in Apple Cider-Vinegar Butter
Sooke Harbour House, Vancouver Island   Courtesy: Chef Pia Carroll
Serves 2

This recipe was inspired by one entitled *"Huitres au beurre du vinaigre de cidre"* appearing in *Bon Appetit* Magazine

1 dozen	oysters
1/4 cup	apple cider (dry)
2 tsp	cider vinegar
1/4 cup	fish stock
1	small shallot, minced
1/2	leek stalk, white part only, minced
1/2 tsp	seaweed, dried (alaria, if possible)
2 tbsp	whipping cream
1/3 cup	cold, unsalted butter, cut into 1/2 in cubes
Garnish	1 tsp finely cut chives

Shuck the oysters over a bowl to catch the liquor. Set aside and reserve the deep half of the shell for serving.

Drain the oysters' liquor into a saucepan. Add apple cider, vinegar, fish stock, shallot, leek and seaweed. Bring to a boil, add the oysters and, depending on their thickness, poach for one minute on each side. Remove from the saucepan and keep warm.

Warm the shells in a covered pan of hot water.

Add cream to the liquid in the saucepan. Bring to a boil and cook until reduced by half and thickened — approximately four minutes.

Whisk in the butter cubes. Remove the warmed shells from the pan, dry and arrange on a serving platter. Place the oysters in each shell and pour the sauce over them. Sprinkle with chives and serve immediately.

Note: If oyster shells are not available, puff pastry shells can be used as an attractive substitute.

A Shot in the Mouth

Drain each **oyster** of its liquid and plop it, dispassionately, into a shot glass of chilled **vodka**. Add a **dash of Tabasco** and gulp down.

As a variation, passed along to us by a well-known restaurateur, add a **teaspoon of vodka** to each **oyster in its shell** and sprinkle with **freshly ground pepper**.

Recommended Wines

European

Chablis
Frascati
Muscadet
Mosel Riesling
Coteau Champenois
Pinot Blanc
Vinho Verde
Gruener Veltliner
Entre-Deux-Mers
Champagne (dry)

North American

Chardonnay
  Washington/New York
Sauvignon Blanc
Riesling
Aligoté
Ravat (dry)
sparkling wine (dry)

The Magic Oyster

Recipes

Steak and Oyster Pie

Courtesy: Chef Chris McNulty

Serves 4

1 1/4 lbs	stewing beef
2 tbsp	vegetable oil
2	onions, chopped
2 tbsp	flour
2 cups	beef stock
	salt and pepper to taste
8	oysters, shucked
1/2 lb	short-crust puff pastry

Remove fat and sinew from the beef and dice into 3/4 in cubes. Heat oil and sauté together with the onions for three or four minutes or until the meat has sealed. Make a roux, by first adding the flour and cooking it for two to three minutes. Then add the stock, mix well and bring to a boil. Season with salt and pepper.

Simmer for 1 1/2 – 2 hours over low heat until the meat is tender. Transfer to a pie dish or to individual small oven-proof dishes. Allow to cool for about one hour.

Preheat oven to 450°F. Place the shucked oysters on top of the meat. Roll out the pastry, making it into a circle large enough to cover the pie dish. Trim and crimp the edges. Use the cut-off strips to decorate the pie.

Egg wash the top and bake the pie (25 – 30 minutes) until the crust is golden brown. Serve immediately.

Note: As a variation, replace the beef stock with half a bottle of Guinness beer.

Fried Oysters
Serves 4

2 cups	oysters, shucked
	oil for frying
5 tbsp	water or milk
2	eggs, beaten
1 cup	unseasoned bread crumbs
1 tsp	salt
1 1/4 tsp	ground pepper
Garnish	lemon wedges

Drain the oysters and dry on paper towels. Add the water or milk to the beaten eggs and stir briskly. Place the bread crumbs, salt and pepper into a sturdy paper bag. Shake well. Dip the oysters into the egg mixture then drop them, a few at a time, into the bag. Roll it around on the counter top until the oysters are completely covered with crumbs.

To a large skillet or iron frying pan, add oil 1/4 in deep. Heat until very hot but not smoking. Add the breaded oysters, a few at a time, making sure they are not touching. Fry one or two minutes on each side until nicely browned and heated through.

Garnish with the lemon wedges and serve with tartar sauce on the side.

The Magic Oyster

Favorite

The Magic Oyster

Oyster Pan Roast
Grand Central Oyster Bar, New York City
Serves 1

The Grand Central Oyster Bar is world famous. Many visitors to New York come to the restaurant just to have this dish and to watch the chefs prepare it individually in just one minute.

8	freshly opened oysters
1 tbsp	butter
1 tbsp	chili sauce
1 tsp	Worcestershire sauce
1/4 cup	oyster liquor
dash	of celery salt
1/2 cup	heavy cream
1	slice dry toast
Garnish	1/2 tsp paprika with 1 tbsp butter

Place all ingredients except cream and toast in the top part of a double boiler over boiling water. Don't let the top pan touch the water.

Whisk or stir briskly and constantly for about one minute, until the oysters are just beginning to curl.

Add the cream and, continuing to stir briskly, bring almost to the boil. Do not boil.

Place the dry toast in the bottom of a soup plate and pour the pan roast over it. Top with the butter and sprinkle with paprika.

The Grand Central Oyster Bar also serves other individual pan roasts and stews.

In each recipe, simply substitute the following for the oysters:

Shrimp
Use 8 or 9   raw shrimps, shelled, deveined, and with tails on

Clam
Use 8 or 9   freshly opened Cherrystone or Littleneck clams

Lobster
Use 1/4lb   fresh lobster meat

Scallop
Use 10 or 12   raw Bay Scallops

Recipes

Oyster Stew
Grand Central Oyster Bar, New York City
Serves 1

Although preparation time is the same and the ingredients for this individually pre-pared and equally popular dish are almost identical to those used in the Oyster Pan Roast, its taste is subtly different.

8	freshly opened oysters
1 tbsp	butter
1/4 cup	oyster liquor
dash	of celery salt
1 tsp	Worcestershire sauce
1 oz	clam juice
1 cup	half-and-half cream
Garnish	1 tbsp butter, 1/2 tsp paprika

Place all the ingredients except the cream in the top part of a double boiler over boiling water. Don't let the top pan touch the water.

Whisk or stir briskly and constantly for about one minute, until oysters are just beginning to curl.

Add the cream and bring almost to a boil, continuing to stir briskly. Do not boil.

Pour the stew into a soup plate. Serve piping hot topped with the butter and sprinkled with paprika.

The Grand Central Oyster Bar also serves other individual pan roasts and stews.

In each recipe, simply substitute the following for the oysters:

Shrimp

Use 8 or 9   raw shrimps, shelled, deveined, and with tails on

Clam

Use 8 or 9   freshly opened Cherrystone or Littleneck clams.

Lobster

Use 1/4lb   fresh lobster meat

Scallop

Use 10 or 12   raw Bay Scallops

Mussel

Only Mussel Stew (no Pan Roast) is served at The Oyster Bar.
Use 14 to 15   mussels, bearded and in the shell.
Omit paprika from this recipe.

Combination

Use   3 shrimp, 2 oysters, 2 clams, 3 scallops, 2 oz lobster meat

Mussels Galore

In Dublin's Fair City

In Dublin's fair city the girls are so pretty,
'Twas there I first met my sweet Molly Malone.
She wheeled her wheelbarrow through the streets broad and narrow,
Crying "cockles and mussels, alive, alive, oh!"

She was a fishmonger, and sure 'twas no wonder,
For so were her mother and father also.
They each wheeled their barrow through the streets broad and narrow,
Crying "cockles and mussels, alive, alive, oh!"

Our First Experience with mussels was daunting. There we were in the south of France, in a magnificent villa near Grasse. The cook had managed to snag a five-kilo bag of mussels for our lunch. We sat down at a table laden with fresh crusty bread, sweet butter and several bottles of local white wine. At first we were merely faint from hunger but, when the cook brought a huge cauldron of steamed mussels into the dining room, we practically swooned as the scent reached our nostrils.

After she had ladled the mussels, together with the fragrant liquid, into our bowls, we nervously watched the other guests as they speared them with their forks and then dipped them into the steaming broth. To our astonishment, the forks were soon abandoned and we discovered that it was *de rigueur* at our table to use the first mussel shell as the tool for extracting the meat from the rest. It seemed logical, so we joined our companions and got our hands wonderfully gooey sopping up the sauce with chunks of great bread.

That memorable meal set the standard for all our future mussel eating. What we needed was some wine, garlic, herbs, and mussels quickly steamed in the broth and served immediately. As novice devotees of these dark blue beauties, we prowled all over the south of France in pursuit of more of the same. We found there were no limits to their adaptability; we had them stuffed, fried, in hot and cold salads, in soups or stews, as starters, main courses and as late-night snacks. Once, in an obscure little Paris restaurant where the mussels were so fantastic, we simply ordered the waiter to keep bringing them until we told him to stop.

That was many years ago, of course, and, since then, mussels have caught on in North America. There is hardly a restaurant serving "continental cuisine" that doesn't offer them as a starter, and the many bistros that have sprung up in the past five years have at least one mussel dish on their menus. Once a week, a favorite of ours features an all-you-can-eat mussel day which attracts large local crowds every Tuesday.

In Times Gone By ...

Long before the white man came to North America, the Indian saltwater tribes who inhabited the coast of the Pacific Northwest knew about the Red Tide, a natural phenomenon that occurs cyclically and causes a concentration of harmful organisms in the ocean. As these tribes lived solely off the products of the sea, they had learned to recognize the luminescent virus which spread an eerie glow on the surface of the sea when it multiplied and its numbers became dangerously high. The Indians would not eat mussels during that time, and even posted guards along the trails to warn off those who lived further inland. But when the luminescence disappeared and the sea turned dark once again, they told them it was safe to harvest these delicious creatures. There also are stories about Acadians who were driven from their homes by the English in the winter of 1755. Desperate for food, they tore mussels from the rocks and ate them. They showed great courage, knowing they were consuming an almost forbidden food. For many years, the huge piles of mussel shells they left behind, served as a monument to their plight.

Perhaps it was the cases of paralytic shellfish or mussel poisoning, recorded along the British Columbia coast as early as 1793, that for so long made the mussel a culinary outsider in North American kitchens. Europeans had enjoyed their delicious taste for centuries and, it is said, when the vassals of the German Emperor Frederick I, also called Barbarossa, wanted to curry favor with their red-bearded monarch, they would appear before him, their shields piled high with mussels.

The mussel's popularity is partly due to our recent health consciousness. It is the only shellfish that is low in cholesterol and fats and high in calcium content. Much like oysters they are easily digested and have the same amount of protein, twice as much phosphorus, iron, thiamine and riboflavin, and an average serving contains one quarter as many calories as a 100-gram steak.

Another reason why this once obscure animal is now so well received is the introduction of modern mussel farming which was an important business as long ago as 500 B.C. The fishermen of Taranto in Italy would harvest mussel crops by lowering ropes or tree branches into the water. The accommodating mussels would attach themselves to these projections and, once the ropes or branches were fully encrusted, the fishermen merely had to pull them out of the water. The ancient Gauls cultivated mussels even before the Romans arrived and it didn't take the Romans long to catch on to the practice.

Although mussel farms have existed in Spain, Portugal and France for the past thirty years, in took an Irishman named Patrick Walton to start the first one in France. It happened quite by accident, as he had, actually, set out to net flying sea birds. He caught few birds but soon noticed that the heavy ropes, called *buchots*, he had used as traps were encrusted with mussels. To harvest his newly discovered crop, Walton built a flat-bottomed boat — an açon — which made it easy to navigate the shallow waters.

Mussel farming came to North America a few short decades ago but, since then, has made abundant supplies available for our consumption. Today, one acre produces about five tons of live mussels or over 4,000 lbs (1,800 kg) of meat annually.

Unlike other shellfish, mussels thrive in the intertidal zone, the area between the high and low tides, where few other sea creatures can survive. We are most familiar with *mytilus edulis*, the common blue variety, which is abundant all along our Atlantic coast. Although it prefers the cold waters between the Arctic and Cape Hatteras, *mytilus edulis* has been introduced to the Pacific west coast where it is doing very well. *Mytilus Californianus*, which is found from Alaska to Mexico, also has been cultivated but with less success. It is larger and much more orange in color than the east-coast variety, though no one is quite sure why that is so.

Mussels have extremely prolific sex lives. Their most important spawn is in May, a lesser one occurring in early fall. A single female can spew out up to 15 million ova in one single spawning and the male isn't far behind in servicing them with sperm. Once fertilized, the eggs become impenetrable.

As every mussel spawns at the same time, the sea becomes cloudy with bobbing eggs. The microscopic larvae, known at this stage as spat, bubble up and down the water in search of food. The spat's wild and free life continues for about three weeks; after that time, it looks for a place to settle down and mature. It generally finds a hard surface or rock and, having anchored itself with its suction-cup foot, it can weather even the heaviest seas.

The mussel exudes a fibrous, sticky substance — the byssus thread — a tuft of brown filaments we call the beard. Because of its adhesive strength, engineers at one time, used mussels as bridge supports by placing them in the spaces between the stones. As the byssus threads attached themselves so firmly, the swiftly moving waters were prevented from washing away the mortar and the bridge could withstand even the most savage weather. In ancient times, these threads also were woven into gloves for Mediterranean fishermen. When not in use, they had to be kept in water so they would not dry out. These gloves were so durable that they were handed down from generation to generation.

The mussel is a filter feeder that processes from ten to fifteen gallons of water a day. It closes its shell tightly at low tide and opens it again slightly when the water covers it. It takes in plankton, along with other minute organic particles including the pollutants present in the water. Although the toxins do not necessarily kill the mussel, they can make other animals, especially people, very sick.

Fresh-water mussels are also good to eat. However, in the United States they have been mainly exploited for making buttons from the mother-of-pearl linings of their shells. Sometimes, they were also induced to produce pearls but the yield was too small to make these ventures commercially successful. Technically, any mussel can produce a pearl but, we are told by Maritimers, it only happens if there are eider ducks around.

How to Gather Mussels in the Wild

Mussels are at their most succulent between October and May. The meat is off-season during both spawning seasons and during the warm summer months.

Before harvesting, check with local authorities to make sure conditions are safe. At low tide, pick those mussels that are closest to the water's edge. They will have spent more time in the water and likely be plumper than others.

How to Buy, Prepare and Store Mussels

Mussels can live up to ten days after leaving the farm. Therefore, it's a good idea to eat them within twenty-four hours after bringing them home from your local fish store. You can spot a wild mussel by the amount of muck it has imbibed, as floating sand and other debris will have gone through it. Almost none of this is present in cultivated mussels.

Sort the mussels by giving each one a good tap. The live ones should immediately close up tightly. If you can rub the shells together without total resistance, assume they are dead and throw them out. The live ones will open up with a change in temperature — when you take them from the refrigerator or from under a cool rinse. Either can be proof of life or death. You can open mussels in a microwave oven set on high for about three minutes.

Once you have accumulated all the live ones, leave them alone as much as possible until you are ready to eat them. Then scrub them with a stiff brush under cold, running water. Remove the beards by pulling away the byssus threads. Scrape off the barnacles or any other surface encrustations.

There are two schools of thought about rinsing mussels. According to the first, add one or two tablespoons of corn meal to the water and let them sit in this solution for at least two hours. This will displace any grit they may contain. The other school holds that it is better to put them through four or five changes of cold-water rinses within about an hour. We prefer the latter method.

Do not keep commercially frozen and shucked mussels in your freezer for longer than four months.

Mussels Galore

Recipes

Mussel Soup
Serves 4

2 lbs	mussels, scrubbed
1	medium onion, chopped
1	celery stalk, chopped
1 1/2 tbsp	parsley, chopped
1 tsp	thyme
pinch	of cayenne pepper, salt and freshly ground black pepper to taste
1 1/2 cups	dry white wine
2 1/2 cups	fish stock
2 tbsp	butter
1 cup	heavy cream
1	egg yolk, lightly beaten
2 tbsp	chives, chopped (optional)

In a large kettle or stock pot, combine onion, parsley, celery, thyme, cayenne pepper, salt and pepper. Add wine, fish stock and butter. Cook over moderate heat until the vegetables are tender.

Add the mussels, cover the pot and bring to the boil. Reduce heat and simmer until the mussels have opened — about five to ten minutes. Do not overcook.

When cool enough to handle, remove the mussels from the shell, discarding those that have remained closed. Set aside.

Puree the vegetables and broth in a blender or food processor. Return to the pot and add mussels, cream and egg yolk. Reheat only long enough for the soup to thicken slightly, stirring constantly.

Serve hot, or cold sprinkled with the chives.

Steamed Mussels or *Moules Marinières*
Serves 4

This is a classic recipe and the most popular and simplest method for cooking mussels.

5 lbs	mussels, scrubbed and shucked
1/4 cup	butter
1	onion, finely chopped, or
1	leek, white part only, chopped
1/2 cup	white wine
1 tsp	parsley
1 tsp	thyme
1 tsp	dried tarragon or fresh basil
1	bay leaf

In a large pot, melt the butter and gently sauté the onion or leek. When transparent, add wine and herbs. Bring to a boil and add enough mussels to fill the pot about two-thirds full. Cover, reduce heat, and steam gently for five to seven minutes. Shake the pot from time to time to make sure the mussels are cooking evenly. Discard any that have remained closed.

Transfer the opened mussels to heated bowls and ladle the hot broth over them. If there is sand on the bottom of the pot, strain the liquid and reheat; however, we like it straight from the pot.

All the mussel devotees we know do variations on this recipe. Those who like spicy *moules marinières*, add a hit of hot sauce; others substitute shallots for the onion or leek. To produce a fine sauce for spaghetti, add some red wine, puréed or chopped tomatoes, basil, parsley and a little lemon juice.

Mussels Galore

Mussels on the Half Shell

As a starter, **two dozen mussels** will serve two to four; as a main course, **allow fourteen to eighteen per person**, if small; **one dozen per person**, if large.

Place the **steamed mussels** in water or wine until ready for use, to prevent a hard crust from forming.

Remove the top shell and add your **favorite stuffing** or a **sautéed** mince of onion, parsley, garlic and dried bread crumbs. **Spread over each mussel** and **broil** until lightly browned.

Recommended Wines

European

Chablis
Frascati
Muscadet
Mosel Riesling
Côteau Champenois
Pinot Blanc
Vinho Verde
Gruener Veltliner
Entre-Deux-Mers
Champagne (dry)

North American

Chardonnay
 Washington/New York
Sauvignon Blanc
Riesling
Aligoté
Ravat (dry)
sparkling wine (dry)

In Praise of the Scallop

Good St. Jacques, rest content, did you really invent
This most succulent poem in fish?
I'm not often this keen on anything piscine
But here is my dream of a dish.

– D. R. Percy – Winner of the New Statesman's
competition for a song in praise of any cooked fish

The Praises of the Scallop have been sung in Greek mythology and the beauty of its shell admired by the great painters of the Renaissance. As a decorative detail, it has adorned ancient humble vessels as well as glorious architectural masterpieces. Because of its extraordinary range of colors, it has fascinated collectors, jewelry makers, architects and furniture designers for many centuries. Apart from all these virtues, it also is one of the tastiest shellfish to eat.

No other story has made the scallop shell more famous than the one about the Shrine of St. Santiago de Compastela in northern Spain which became a favorite place of pilgrimage in the twelfth century. It is said that it was here where James the Apostle made several attempts to convert the heathens to Christianity. Although he was unsuccessful, the challenge was so great that he returned time and again. He eventually died in the little town and when the news leaked out in 850 A.D. that he was buried there, the faithful came to pay homage to him. The trek started, of course, on the *rue Saint-Jacques* in Paris. This is a custom that hasn't died out.

Despite the fact that Santiago de Compastela was twelve miles from the sea, it was customary for pilgrims to attach scallop shells to the hems of their garments as proof that they had visited the important shrine.

According to another legend, a transplanted heathen Mayan lord was at the head of his wedding procession when his horse bolted and fell into the coastal water off Galicia, a province in northwestern Spain. With its master on its back, the horse swam to a nearby ship that happened to be carrying the body of St. James. By the time horse and rider returned to shore, they both were covered with scallop shells. Convinced that a miracle had occurred, the Mayan chieftain converted to Christianity.

In honor of the redoubtable *Saint-Jacques*, the scallop shell became the universal symbol of the weary traveller and, by 1150, was incorporated in the designs of numerous stained glass windows and cathedral façades.

The most familiar use in art of the scallop shell is, of course, Botticelli's *Venus Rising*, showing the goddess on a half shell, modestly concealing herself behind her long hair. In earlier periods, many other Venuses rose from the opalescent shell, such as the one depicted on the earthen-ware jug now on display in the Hermitage Museum in Leningrad. Dating back to 400 B.C., it is considered one of the oldest representations of the birth of Venus from a shell.

It is difficult to establish exactly when the scallop became a popular food. In the fifteenth century, the *éschalope* was brought to the English court by the French, who had derived the word from *écale*, meaning pea pod, nut shell, hull or husk. The English changed it to scallop, later expanding its meaning to include the ornamental "scalloped" edges on cloth and lace, as well as the dishes baked with bread crumbs or in a cream sauce.

There are about three hundred species of scallops, all of them edible. The most familiar among them are the Atlantic Bay and the Sea Scallops. The smaller Bay measuring about 3 in (7 cm) in diameter loves to spend its life among eel-grass close to the shore. The commercially more valuable Sea Scallop which grows to approximately 8 in (20 cm) in diameter is caught further off shore. Comparable species exist on the Pacific coast and are being introduced to new areas in Canada — the Bay Scallop to Prince Edward Island and the "Singing" or Vancouver Scallop to British Columbia, where it is being farmed and exported to the Seattle area in Washington State.

Scallops are the perkiest of all the bivalves. They move as if jet-propelled throughout the ocean world. You can imitate their movements by blowing out of different sides of your mouth, which is what these animals do as they dash about the ocean in different directions. The reason for such urgent motion, is the peculiar structure of the scallop's body which has also created the shape of its shell. It is light, reinforced with fluting radiating outward from the hinge, and must withstand the heavy pressure of its deep-water habitat. In the Pacific Ocean, some have been found at depths of 2,000 fathoms or 12,000 feet (3,657 meters).

The scallop has about fifty eyes, each equipped with a cornea, a lens and an optic nerve, but set in the opposite direction to which the shell is headed. Spectacular as these two rows of orbs may be, peering out from an almost closed shell, they cannot perceive anything except movement and light.

The scallop only has one large adductor muscle — the one that opens and closes the shell — instead of the bivalves' usual two. Since it cannot completely close its mouth, it dies soon after it is taken from the sea.

How to Gather Scallops in the Wild

Scallops have no specific season but if you can find fresh ones, they are at their best from April to October. The essence of a real scallop treat is to allow the least time to elapse between shore and stove. Some of our acquaintances like to pick scallops out of the water and pop them right into their mouths — as is. Most people tell us they prefer to take them back to the cottage and eat them dipped in hot melted butter.

How to Buy Scallops

Scallops are available both fresh and frozen all year round. They should smell sweet and their flesh should be creamy white, light tan or just, slightly pink. The commercial fishermen who harvest them usually remove the adductor muscle and discard the coral (roe) and the innards. However, if you can get your hands on some freshly caught ones, be sure to try the whole animal and certainly the delicious coral. Buy your scallops from reliable fish merchants. Unscrupulous vendors make fakes from cheap shark meat they cut into scallop shapes with cookie-cutters and then sell at premium prices.

When buying frozen scallops, look for packages that contain no excess liquid.

How to Shuck Scallops

Insert a strong implement, such as a dinner knife, between the two shell halves, near the hinge. Twist but do not force the shell open. To sever the muscle from the top shell, lift it up far enough to get inside with the knife, leaving it attached to the bottom half. Remove the gray viscera and discard. Pull to retrieve the white part and the roe. Now cut the muscle from the shell and wash it under cold, running water.

How to Cook Scallops

Scallops have a low fat content and are high in protein and niacin. Treat these subtly flavored, delicate little creatures gently, as overcooking can turn them rubbery. The simpler the preparation method the better.

Cooking Times in Minutes

	Bay Scallops	Sea Scallops		Bay Scallops	Sea Scallops
Poaching	2	4	Baking	5 – 8	4
Sautéing	2	2 – 3	Deep Frying	1 – 2	2 – 3
Broiling	2 – 3	3 – 4	Stir Frying	1 – 2	2 – 3
Stewing	2	4			

Poached Scallops
Serves 4

Poaching in a light court bouillon is one of the best ways to cook scallops.

1/2 cup	white wine to **2 cups** water, or
1/4 cup	wine vinegar to **2 cups** water
1	carrot, scraped and thinly sliced
1	onion, thinly sliced
1	leek, white part only, sliced
1	rib celery, sliced
1 lb	scallops, shucked

Add the vegetable slices to the liquid and bring to a gentle rolling boil. Add the scallops and simmer for five minutes.

Recipes

Digby Sea Scallops Sautéed in Garlic and Sherry
Filet of Sole Restaurant, Toronto   Courtesy: Chef Kee Lee

2 lbs	fresh or frozen Digby Sea Scallops
1 cup	flour for coating
4 tbsp	unsalted butter
4 tbsp	olive oil
2 – 3	cloves garlic, finely chopped
	salt and freshly ground pepper to taste
1 – 2 tbsp	dry sherry
Garnish	chopped parsley

Wash and dry scallops. If frozen, make sure they are completely thawed. Toss them in flour until lightly coated. Shake off excess flour.

In a skillet, heat butter and olive oil. Add garlic and scallops, stirring and tossing quickly. Add sherry and season with salt and pepper.

The scallops are cooked when they turn opaque. Avoid overcooking, since it will toughen these tasty morsels.

Just before serving, sprinkle with enough parsley to coat the scallops.

Serve over buttered rice pilaf.

Scallops à la Canepa

Tadich Grill, San Francisco   Courtesy: Chef John Canepa

Serves 2

18	medium scallops
1 tbsp	flour
2 tbsp	olive oil
4 oz	butter
3 tbsp	onion, chopped
pinch	of salt, cayenne pepper and nutmeg
2 oz	Chardonnay or Chablis
6 oz	whipping cream
1 /2 cup	sour cream
1 tbsp	chives, finely chopped
1 tsp	parsley, chopped
juice	of 1 lemon

Drain scallops. Dust well with flour.

In a skillet, heat oil and 2 oz butter to medium temperature. Add scallops, cooking and turning them until lightly browned. Add seasoning and sauté for two minutes. Add wine and cook a little longer until reduced. Add whipping cream and gently simmer for four minutes.

Remove from heat and stir in sour cream, chives, parsley, remaining solid butter and lemon juice.

Serve immediately with buttered noodles and vegetables on the side.

In Praise of the Scallop

Recipes

Fricassée of Scallops and Artichokes

Courtesy: Chef Patrick Desmoulins

Serves 4

1	carrot, diced
1	celery stalk, diced
1/4 lb	unsalted butter
20 oz	fresh scallops
8	fresh artichoke hearts, cooked and quartered
juice	of 2 lemons
1 tbsp	white wine
1 tbsp	chopped chives
	salt and pepper to taste

In a saucepan steam carrot and celery until *al dente*. Set aside.

Melt 2 tablespoons of the butter in a frying pan. Add scallops and artichoke hearts and sauté over medium to high heat for two minutes. Transfer to a warmed round platter.

To make the sauce, deglaze the frying pan with lemon juice and white wine until reduced by half. Add remaining butter and the steamed vegetables. Sprinkle with chives and swirl the pan away from the heat to allow the butter to coat the mixture. Do not over heat. Add salt and pepper to taste.

Arrange the artichoke hearts in the center of the platter. Surround them with the scallops to form a broken circle.

Spoon the sauce on top and serve.

Baked Scallops
Serves 4

2 lbs	scallops, shucked and quartered
1 tbsp	lemon juice
1/8 cup	white wine
1 tbsp	butter
1/4 cup	table cream
Topping	bread crumbs, melted butter

Preheat oven to 400°F. In a bowl, toss the scallops, together with lemon juice and white wine.

Melt butter in a shallow baking dish. Add scallop mixture and cream.

Sprinkle with bread crumbs and dribble melted butter on top.

Bake for twelve to fourteen minutes.

Recommended Wines

European

Chablis
Frascati
Muscadet
Mosel Riesling
Côteau Champenois
Pinot Blanc
Vinho Verde
Gruener Veltliner
Entre-Deux-Mers
Champagne (dry)

North American

Chardonnay
    Washington/New York
Sauvignon Blanc
Riesling
Aligoté
Ravat (dry)
sparkling wine (dry)

In Praise of the Scallop

Clams-Clams-Clams

"Inglorious friend! Most confident I am
Thy life is one of very little ease;
Albeit men mock thee with their smiles
And prate of being "happy as a clam!"

– John G. Saxe

Of all the Bivalves, none is known by more names nor lends itself to more preparation methods than the clam. Say Steamer, Longneck, Ipswich, Wampum, Squirt or Belly and, depending on where you live, you are talking about a soft-shell clam. Hard shells are called quahogs which, in turn, are variously known as Littlenecks, Cherrystones (Cherries), Mediums, Bay Quahogs or Chowder Clams; Bar or Surf Clams, also called Skimmers, Hen or Sea Clams, are found along the Atlantic coast — from Labrador via the Gulf of St. Lawrence to the Gulf of Mexico.

The clam is equipped with a powerful, tongue-shaped foot at the opposite end of its neck or siphon. By expanding and contracting the foot, it is able to burrow, with surprising speed, into the sandy ocean shallows it calls home. Clams also are dioecious which means that, unlike oysters, they have separate sexes.

The things you can do with clams! You can steam them, fry them, bake them or eat them raw. You can use them in chowders, in bisques, in stews, in rich pan roasts and in creamy pies. They can be made into fritters and clam cakes and, for those who like them totally disguised, into clam dips. Finally, the briny juice of the clam, when chilled on its own or mixed with tomato juice, becomes the silent vodka's spicy companion in a Bloody Caesar.

While some intrepid souls insist that any clam can be devoured raw, others consider the chewy, briny hard shell we call quahog a treat equal to that of raw oysters. For these devotees, the perfect place is, in fact, a "raw bar" where they can spend the afternoon alternating clams and oysters to their hearts' content, and washing them down with an ample flow of cold draft beer or chilled white wine.

The all-time quahog favorites sold at these shellfish bars are the Littlenecks which are just plain "Necks" to their biggest boosters. Measuring no more than 2 1/4 in across, they are, by far, the tenderest and sweetest of all the hard shells.

The next size up are the Cherrystones. To claim that name, they must range in size from 2 1/4 in to 3 in across the width of their shells. While preferred by raw-clam aficionados because of their chewiness, some restaurateurs use them for baked-clam appetizers, while others have been known to pass them off as the more expensive Littlenecks. If you're not sure what they are and want to impress your friends, pull out your caliper and measure the little rascals in their shells!

Throughout much of New England, quahogs measuring more than 3 in across are known as Chowder Clams because they usually are chopped up or minced for use in chowders.

The meat of Bar or Surf Clams also can be minced and often appears in canned and frozen clam products. Abundant in Canadian waters, these clams are harvested from clean, gravely sand bars at low tide.

The Ocean Quahogs — "O-Q' s" — also known as Black or Mahogany Clams, are half-pound cousins of the Surfs. They live in sandy mud, further off shore, at depths ranging from 100 – 250 feet. Keeping up the ever increasing demands of the clamming industry, they have become a valuable source of meat to supplement the harvest from traditional Surf Clam beds. While the O-Q's meat is too dark to be used in the creamy-colored New England chowders, it is ideal for the Manhattan variety, as well as for products such as clam sticks, stuffed clams and clam pies.

The Razor Clam is an oddity not commonly found on restaurant menus or in retail stores. With its long, thin shell measuring up to 10 in in length and looking like an old-fashioned straight razor's handle or blade holder, it is said to be very sweet and chewy when steamed.

Finally, there are the monsters of the Pacific Ocean — the Horse Clams with a shell measuring upward of 8 in across, and the giant Geoduck (pronounced, gooey-duck) whose name stems from the west-coast Indian word meaning "digging deep." Tipping the scale at twelve pounds, these extraordinary clams live in sandy beds, sixty to eighty feet below the surface of the sea. To harvest them, divers must use high-pressure hoses to blow away the sand that covers them in their hiding places.

How to Buy and Clean Clams

Hand pick soft-shell as well as hard-shell clams as you would oysters. Reject those with cracked or gaping shells that do not close quickly when handled. Allow approximately one dozen per person and, for good measure, add another dozen to the pot.

To remove sand, mud and grit, scrub hard shells with a stiff brush under cold running water. Clean the more brittle shells of soft-shell clams under cold running water by hand.

Despite the purists' warnings that too much washing dilutes the hard shells' natural brininess, some people soak theirs in salted water or water to which salt and several tablespoons of corn meal have been added. They claim that clams immersed in this solution, will clean themselves by "inhaling" the water and "exhaling" the grit.

How to Steam and Serve Clams

Since steamed soft-shell clams are a seaside treat that is also easy to prepare, it is surprising that people don't eat them at home more often.

Fill your steamer or stock pot with 1/2 in of water. Place the scrubbed and cleaned clams into the steamer basket or on a rack in the bottom of the pot. Cover and steam the clams over medium heat until they open — usually five to ten minutes.

After you have finished steaming the clams, strain the liquid left in the bottom of the pot. Pour it into juice glasses but be careful to leave behind the sand. To chill the broth, store it tightly covered in your refrigerator, but for no longer than twelve hours.

Serve in soup bowls, accompanied by a small dish of melted butter, one or two lemon wedges per person, and a juice glass of clam broth in which to dip and "wash" the clams before dipping them in the melted butter.

How to Eat Steamed Clams

"Tourists, mainland and inland folk are squeamish when it comes to clams," say those who live close to the pull of the sea. "What's that?" they squirm when watching their down east host or hostess dip a dangling, bulging Belly into clam juice and melted butter. "Enjoy!" reply those familiar with the etiquette of eating steamed clams ... and eventually they do.

Like lobster, steamed clams are best consumed in the privacy of your home where you can enjoy them in comfort and, likely, at half the price restaurants charge.

There are various ways to eat them: according to etiquette expert Emily Post, it is proper to pick the meat off the shells with a fork which, after removing the "neck" sheath, is used for dipping the meat, first into the broth and then into melted butter, before popping the clam into your mouth in one bite.

The author of *Miss Manners' Guide to Excruciatingly Correct Behaviour* suggests the "fastidious clam eater will take a complete bath after each clam." She, therefore, recommends the more "hands-on" approach of providing each guest with a towel disguised as a napkin and always using a washable tablecloth.

Soft-shell Steamers are finger foods ideally shared by two people, as long as the one doesn't embarrass the other by using a fork. Even if your appetite is bucket sized, order no more than one bucket or bowl at a time, as broth and melted butter cool quickly. The clams will keep hotter and, therefore, taste better if they are not allowed to stand around for too long.

If you are eating steamed clams in a restaurant and find more than a few with unopened shells, don't fuss with them as they are not edible and should be discarded. Instead, bring that fact to the attention of your waiter or waitress who will make sure that the second batch contains a better selection; most good places even throw in a few extras to compensate guests for those that had to be passed up the first time around.

Pick the clam from the bucket or bowl, pinch its neck between thumb and index finger, then pull the entire piece of meat, gently but firmly, from the gaping shell. With your fingers, slip off the black neck sheath. Discard it together with the shell in the receptacle provided for empties.

Holding the clam by its neck, dunk it into the clam juice. This will not only wash away any sand or grit clinging to the body, but also coat the clam with its own rich, tasty liquor. Now dip it into the melted butter and, using the least-likely-to-stain route, plop the whole clam into your mouth. Fussier people, hold half a clam shell under the dripping delicacy to manoeuver it safely from bowl to lips.

Eating clams is a juicy, buttery, sybaritic experience which leaves even the most seasoned enthusiast wet of chin. However, to cope with the sand that comes with it, remember that everyone at your table and around the room (if you are eating in a restaurant) is faced with the same inconvenience. Remove the sand from your mouth in the same way as you would a fish bone or cherry pit-discreetly spitting it into a spoon or a napkin.

Steamed hard-shell clams, usually Cherrystones or Littlenecks, are eaten with a fork. They normally are served by the half or full dozen, with hot melted butter and lemon wedges on the side.

Down-East Clam Chowder
Serves 4

Whether using canned or fresh hard-shell clams, allow approximately one quart clam meat for four people; be sure to save the juice.

1/4 lb	salt pork, diced
1	large onion, diced
3	medium potatoes, peeled and diced (about **2 cups**)
4 cups	liquid (**2 1/2 cups** whole milk to **1 1/2 cups** clam juice plus potato water)
1/2	bay leaf
1 quart	shucked clams, including their juice (if using Cherrystones or quahogs, cut in half or quarter)
Garnish	pats of cold butter

In a large stew pot or Dutch oven, fry the pork dices slowly, until brown. Set aside. Sauté the onion in the pork fat until soft and transparent. Set aside.

Add the potatoes and enough water to rise about 1 in (2 1/2 cm) above them in the pot. Boil for approximately ten minutes. They should be cooked yet firm.

Drain and reserve potato water. Add enough to the clam juice to yield two cups.

Add the reserved salt pork, the onion and the bay leaf to the pot. Heat slowly then stir in the milk. Add the clams, reduce heat and simmer for ten to twelve minutes.

Before serving, add pats of butter to each bowl. Allow your guests to salt and pepper to taste.

Recipes

Fried Clams
Serves 4

Clams, of course, have been around since the tide came in, but, say the custodians of folklore, fried clams were invented in 1916 by the founder of Woodman's of Essex, Massachusetts, one of New England's most popular shellfish eateries.

24	soft-shell clams (6 per serving)
1	egg, lightly beaten
2 tsp	water
1 tsp	milk
2 cups	fine dry bread crumbs butter and oil for frying

Scrub and shuck the clams, making certain to remove the skin that covers the neck of the clam and the membrane around the edge of the shell. Dry them on paper towels.

Holding each clam by the neck, dunk it into the egg-water-milk mixture, then roll it in the bread crumbs. Heat the fat — half butter, half oil — and sauté the clams until golden brown.

Serve with tartare sauce on the side.

Favorite Recipes

Clams Casino
Serves 4

1	clove garlic, minced
2 tbsp	parsley, chopped
1/4 cup	butter
3 tbsp	white wine
1/2 cup	fresh bread crumbs
1/2 cup	Romano cheese, grated bacon slices cut into 24 – 1 in squares
24	Littleneck or Cherrystone clams (6 per serving)

Combine garlic and parsley with melted butter. Add white wine.

Combine bread crumbs and cheese.

To keep the clam shells from wobbling or tipping over, cover a cookie sheet with crumpled foil. Place the clams on the half shell on the foil. Top each with the bread crumb-cheese mixture and dribble the garlic butter-wine mixture on top.

Place one bacon square on each clam.

Broil until the bacon is done and the crumb topping has nicely browned.

Manhattan Clam Chowder

This recipe is almost identical to the Down-East Clam Chowder with the following changes:

1. Omit the milk. Instead, use the clam juice-potato-water mixture to make up the four cups of liquid.

2. While the chowder is cooking, add **3 cups** cooked or canned tomatoes, **1/4 cup** catsup, **1** small diced green pepper, **2** tablespoons butter and, finally, the clams.

Recommended Wines

European

Chablis
Frascati
Muscadet
Mosel Riesling
Côteau Champenois
Pinot Blanc
Vinho Verde
Gruener Veltliner
Entre-Deux-Mers
Champagne (dry)

North American

Chardonnay
   Washington/New York
Sauvignon Blanc
Riesling
Aligoté
Ravat (dry)
sparkling wine (dry)

Clams-Clams-Clams

The Squid and the Octopus

The Squid-Jiggin' Ground

O this is the place where the fishermen gather,
In oil skins and boots and cape – arms battened down;
All sizes of figures with squid lines and jiggers,
They congregate here on the squid-jiggin' ground.

– A.R. Scammell (BMI Canada Limited)

Our Favorite Squid Story comes from a friend who was visiting a Newfoundland outport many years ago. He recalls:

"We were sitting around drinking rum, lots of rum, when one of the neighborhood fishermen came bursting in about midnight. In his hands he had a squid, just caught. We cut it up and put it in the ice box until the next day.

"My friend put a little garlic in a pan with oil and sautéed the squid for less than two minutes. We sat down to eat it immediately. ... It was one of those memorable moments. It's sweet and delicate and I recommend it highly for a hangover.

"The fisherman who had given it to us wouldn't eat it, of course. For him it was strictly bait."

The Squid

The folklore that surrounds this animal is mostly of the "loony-moon" kind or the terrifying stories people tell of fishermen being attacked by squids, sucked down into the briny deep and held prisoner by their rasping tentacles. Science fiction writers also have had them growing to unbelievable proportions, such as the giant squid that attacked Captain Nemo and his crew in the Nautilus (*Twenty Thousand Leagues Under The Sea*) — a nice inside joke since the nautilus is related to the squid, the octopus, and the cuttlefish.

This "head-footed" mollusk has a distinct head from which spring arms and tentacles, equipped with powerful suckers; two large eyes sit on either side of the head. It is one of two cephalopods that has retained an external shell which attests to its prehistoric past when squids were gigantic creatures and considered the rulers of the sea.

Squids come in various sizes. They can be tiny — no bigger than your thumb; two feet in length, such as the loligo that patrols the coasts of North America, or as long as *Architeuthis princeps* — the largest of all the invertebrates — which can be up to forty-eight feet (14.6m) in length.

The squid also is a decapod, a cephalopod with ten arms of which two are actually tentacles. It can scurry through the ocean by jet propulsion, in any direction it pleases, steered backward or forward by small fins at the rear of its body. A trace of its former shell — the pen or quill — rests inside the body. The slender skeleton running along the dorsal side looks and feels almost like plastic. Inside the body cavity is the famous ink sac which releases a murky fluid. Most authorities believe that the purpose of the ink, when ejected, is to fool the animal's enemies as it creates a cloudy likeness of its body. This allows the squid to steal away, leaving its attacker to battle nothing but an inky specter.

The chromatophores — color-producing cells — embedded in the skin of the squid allow it to blend into its background and react to different situations. If, for instance, a crab comes along, the color will intensify as soon as the squid gets ready for the kill. On the other hand, when it wants to confuse or dazzle an approaching foe, it can turn dark red or brown in a split second.

Squid have more fun in their sex lives than many other mollusks. The Atlantic

Squid (*Illex illecebrosus*), for example, migrates hundreds of miles to spawn in warmer waters. Fertilization takes place in three stages: First, the male penetrates the female and deposits his sperm inside her body. Then the female lays her eggs and squirts them with the sperm. In the third stage, the male squirts more sperm into the water near the eggs which are soft enough to become fertilized. During this great drama, the squids — especially the females — exhaust themselves almost to the point of death. Once the baby squid have hatched, they get away from the mother's nest as quickly as possible. As their first independent act they eject a spurt of ink into their new world.

Squids will eat just about anything they can get their arms on — big fish, small fish, even other squids. They, in turn, are a major food source for dozens of fish, as well as for such mammals as the dolphin. Although squid can elude most of their enemies by squeezing into incredibly tiny spaces, they cannot get away from the eel which follows them to their hide-aways and then attacks with razor-sharp teeth.

The myths about the moon madness of squid are based on truth because, mesmerized by the light of the moon, they surface at night to feed on plankton and fishes; this allows their predators to simply pluck them from the sea. Commercial fishermen now use sonar equipment to locate them during the day; at night they can spot them by shining lights on the water surface. They then are netted and drawn directly into the hold of ships by hydraulic pumps.

The Octopus

There it sits atop a treasure chest of pirates' loot,
The tentacled, grim guardian of the briny deep.
Lurking in the shadow of the hold of a sunken galleon or –
horror of 'horrors – under the bed when the lights go out!
*   – Anonymous*

Most North Americans associate the octopus more with nightmares and monster movies than with fine dining. And that's a pity for, given its diet, it should be the stuff seafood lovers' dreams are made of. In fact, a list of the creature's favorite snacks reads like a menu scribbled on the chalk board outside a seaside shellfish bar: lobster, crab, abalone, oysters and clams.

Like the squid, the octopus is a cephalopod. Its mating habits and the behavior of its young are similar to those of the squid and, when threatened, it uses the same methods to protect itself. The ink-like fluid it ejects forms a cloud that not only acts as an effective smoke screen but also looks sufficiently like an octopus to distract its attackers long enough for it to beat a stealthy retreat across the ocean floor.

Marine biologists also suggest that the ink contains a substance that deadens the olfactory nerves of its enemies, especially those of the moray eel. In the Pacific Ocean, they have actually watched morays bump into octopuses and then swim away without getting as much as a nibble at their favorite food.

Ink sacs aside, the octopus, like its cousin the squid, is well equipped to survive the dangers' of the deep. Its eyes are every bit as good as those of humans' and its mouth, shaped like a parrot's beak, is a strong and perfect ripping tool. It also can take on the colors of its surroundings and, being boneless, is able to squeeze through narrow crevices or hide in places too small for its enemies to enter. Moving about less often than the squid, it swims just as well using the same method of "jet propulsion." Helped along by eight tentacled arms, its physical dexterity is equal to that of chimpanzees or the most athletic of humans. When planning a meal of clams or oysters, it has been seen sneaking pebbles into their gaping shells to prevent them from snapping shut. Also, having grasped a lobster or crab with one or more of its arms, it can immobilize the crustacean even further by injecting it with a venomous fluid that may, we are told, be a form of "spicing," similar to the catsup or Tabasco we use to flavor food.

The main commercial catch consists of *Octopus dofieine* which is harvested in the Pacific while Octopus vulgaris comes from the Atlantic coast. Although these species can grow upwards of forty-five to fifty feet in tentacle span, those which make it to market usually are about a foot long.

The octopus has been with us for some 600 million years — a remarkable feat considering that of the more than 10,000 cephalopods identified in fossil form no more than a handful are around today. When H.G.Wells created his War of the Worlds, he saw the octopus as the logical and superior invader. Given the intelligence of this soft-bodied, strange-looking creature, the vision is not that far-fetched, as many present-day marine biologists believe a land invasion by cephalopods might have been a crucial evolutionary stage.

While we have been shuddering and reaching for our night lights at the mere mention of the octopus' name, people in other countries have been enjoying it for years. In France it is, called *poulpe*, in Spain, *pulpo*; Italians know it as *polpo di scoglio* and, while it is *polvo* to the Portuguese, the Greeks refer to it as *octapodi*. None of these names sound quite as romantic and glamorous as *calamari* — a linguistic disguise which, in no small way, has contributed to the growing popularity of the squid on North American menus.

How to Buy Squid or Octopus

Between sixty and eighty per cent of their meat is edible which makes them good buys; eighteen per cent of that is protein which makes it even better. Although a delicacy as well as a cheap form of nutrition in Mediterranean and Asian countries, on this continent the popularity of both squid and octopus has been negligible, probably because many North Americans are squeamish about anything slimy or slithery.

The edible parts of these animals are the body sac or pouch, the long tentacles and arms and the ink sac. You can purchase squid live, fresh, frozen, salted, pickled, sun-dried and canned. When buying it live, look for a milky translucent color. Fresh, the skin should be creamy-white with reddish brown spots; a pinkish hue is the sign of aging. The meat is white and firm, has little fat and few connective tissues.

Octopuses are not sold live but usually marketed fresh or frozen — dressed or gutted with the eyes removed. Fish dealers gladly perform the task for you if it has not been done, including removal of the ink sac which you can put to good use in many recipes.

Shop carefully for both squid and octopus, as the slightest smell of fishiness should be a warning that the one you selected has seen better days.

How to Prepare Squid

Draw back the rim of the body pouch to remove the shell-like pen; it will come out when head and tentacles are pulled apart. Discard the pen. Holding the head below the eyes, pull the pouch away from the body. Rinse after removing the mucous membrane.

With your fingers, pop out the eye sections and the small round cartilage at the base of the tentacles. Discard. Remove the viscera but, before discarding it, extract the distinctive ink sac which lies near the liver. Be careful not to squeeze it. Reserve.

Gently pull off the translucent skin by sliding your finger under it. From either side of pouch and skin, pull away the edible fins. If the squid is longer than 8 in (20 cm), scrape off the tentacles' sharp-edged suckers with a knife.

Sever the tentacles from the head, just below the eyes. Cut them into rings. Remove the beak by squeezing it out of the fleshy rim. Discard. Reserve the pouch for stuffing or cut it into 2-inch squares.

To firm the flesh, it is customary in countries such as Spain to allow the squid to "rest" (refrigerated) for twelve hours before it is cooked.

How to Prepare Octopus

The preparation method for octopus is identical to that for squid with the following exceptions:

1. The octopus does not have a pen.
2. Since its skin will not slip off as easily as that of the squid, rub some salt into the flesh to loosen it. Peel off the skin by hand, then soak the flesh in cold water for twenty minutes to get rid of the salt. You also can poach the flesh for two minutes in a pot of simmering water before attempting to remove the skin. The octopus' suckers need not be removed.

How to Store Squid or Octopus

Covered with plastic, fresh squid or octopus can be kept in the refrigerator for up to one day. If frozen, thawed and cleaned it must be used immediately.

When dried, soak in water to which a dash of ginger has been added. Proceed in the same way as you would with fresh squid or octopus.

If you have prepared more squid or octopus than you can use immediately, cook the leftovers as per recipe and leave them to cool in a shallow dish. Freeze. Remove the frozen block, wrap and store in your freezer.

How to Cook Squid or Octopus

You can eat them broiled, sautéed, deep-fried, baked, stewed, stir-fried or marinated; they are excellent in salads or pasta sauces and were born to be stuffed. Adding the ink sac to the sauce of any squid or octopus dish will produce a smoother texture and a rich, dark-brown color. To liquefy the ink after it has been frozen, let it dissolve in a little boiling water. A very small squid may have only one or two drops of ink.

Many cookbooks recommend tenderizing the meat. To do so, turn the pouch inside out and pound with a wooden mallet; then turn it right side out and pound again.

If you are planning to stuff the pouch, the Spanish method of dipping the whole animal into boiling water is easier and less likely to split the pouch. Immerse the octopus or squid into boiling water for several seconds. Lift out to cool for a minute or two. Dunk again, this time for four to five seconds.

When cooled after the "second dip, lower into a pot of boiling water, reduce the temperature and simmer for about an hour. The meat will be tender enough for any recipe you have in mind.

Cooking Times

Actually, there are only two cooking times — very short or very long. Both are crucial to the success of the meal. As squid and octopus dry out quickly, fry, sauté, broil or deep fry for no more than one or two minutes. If you go beyond these magic times, it will take a lot of moisture and long, slow cooking to bring the meat back to its tender stage.

Stew squid about twenty to forty-five minutes. For octopus, depending on its size, stewing times can vary between sixty to ninety minutes.

Marinated Squid or Octopus

1/2 cup	virgin olive oil
1/2 cup	white wine
1/4 cup	green onions, white part only, chopped
juice	of 1 lime
meat	from **1 squid** or **octopus**, cut into 2 in squares

Prepare a marinade by combining all the ingredients.
Add the squid or octopus and allow to marinate for eight hours,
turning after four.

Use in salads or sauté in accordance with your favorite recipe.

Sautéed Squid or Octopus

Sauté finely chopped garlic in a combination of oil and butter. Sprinkle with
fresh chopped parsley. Add squid or octopus and sauté for no more than two
minutes.

Broiled Squid or Octopus

Marinate for one hour in olive oil, salt and pepper. Broil over charcoal for
one to two minutes.

The Squid and the Octopus

Favorite

Stuffed Squids
Serves 2 – 4

6	large prepared squids, tender parts of the tentacles, chopped
1/4 cup	bread crumbs, fresh
2 tbsp	parsley, chopped
2 1/2 tbsp	Parmesan cheese, grated
2 tbsp	garlic, finely chopped
1	egg, lightly beaten
1/4 cup	olive oil
	salt and freshly ground pepper
4	whole garlic cloves, peeled
1/2 cup	tomatoes, peeled and chopped
1/4 cup	white wine (dry)
	ink from reserved ink sac (optional)

For the stuffing, place the chopped tentacles in a mixing bowl. Add bread crumbs, parsley, cheese, 1 1/2 teaspoons of the chopped garlic and the beaten egg. Add enough olive oil — about a tablespoon — to make the stuffing glossy. Blend with a fork, adding salt and pepper to taste.

Spoon equal amounts of the mixture into each squid body, being careful not to overstuff as it shrinks during cooking. Sew up the openings with thread or seal with toothpicks.

To make the sauce, heat the remaining oil in a large skillet. Add the garlic cloves and sauté until golden brown. Remove and discard.

The Squid and the Octopus

Add the squids in a single layer. Sauté lightly on both sides. Add the tomatoes, the remaining chopped garlic and the wine. Season with salt and pepper to taste.

Cover and cook twenty to thirty minutes. Lift the squids from the pan. Remove the threads or toothpicks and cut each one crosswise into half-inch slices.

Arrange reassembled on a serving platter. If you wish, add the ink from the reserved ink sac to the sauce. Heat it and pour over the stuffed squids. Serve with rice on the side.

Recipes

Kelp Greenling and Squid

Sooke Harbour House, Vancouver Island   *Courtesy: Chef Michael Stadtlander*

Serves 4

Seafood

1	kelp greenling, boned and cut into four 6-oz portions
1	8-oz whole squid, cleaned
1 oz	butter
	thyme, parsley, tarragon, fennel finely chopped, combined to make 1/2 cup
1 cup	white wine
2 tbsp	lemon juice
1/4 tsp	Worcestershire sauce

Vegetables

1 oz	butter
4	bok choy leaves, washed and left whole
4	Swiss chard leaves, washed and left whole
2	shallots, finely chopped
8	new potatoes, steamed and kept warm

In a large skillet, sauté greenling in hot butter — approximately three minutes on each side, depending on thickness. Remove from pan and keep warm.

Add squid and fresh herbs and sauté until tender. Remove from pan and keep warm.

Add wine, lemon juice and Worcestershire sauce to the pan and cook over high heat until reduced to a glaze. Set aside.

Now the vegetables: melt butter in a large skillet. Add bok choy, Swiss chard and shallots. Sauté briefly.

Arrange greenling and squid on top of the bok choy — Swiss chard leaves divided among four plates. Pour over the glaze. Add two potatoes to each plate and serve immediately.

Recommended Wines

European

Entre-Deux-Mers
Vouvray
Gewuerztraminer
Anjou
Liebfraumilch
Riesling Spaetlese
Riesling
Malvasia

North American

Sylvaner
Vidal
Chenin Blanc
Aurora
Riesling
Orvieto Abboccato

Good Places to Eat Shellfish

The list of seafood restaurants is based on our own experiences, as well as those of friends and colleagues Elizabeth Baird, Tara Baxendale, Jim Bradley, Winston Collins, Margaret Eaton, Jennifer Harris, Joanne Kates, Ann Kemp, Anne Mortimer-Maddox ('Dusty'), Karin and Neil Shakery, Bonnie Stern and Lucy Waverman who all kindly added their suggestions to ours.

We have listed these places alphabetically rather than grading them according to personal preferences.

(Locations marked *seasonal* are generally open late May to October.)

IN CANADA

British Columbia

Vancouver

Beach House Restaurant
150 – 25th Street
West Vancouver
(604) 922-1414

Blue Water Café
1095 Hamilton Street
(604) 688-8078

C Restaurant
1600 Howe Street and False Creek
Waterfront
(604) 681-1164

The Cannery Seafood Restaurant
2205 Commissioner Street
(604) 254-9606

Salmon House on the Hill
2229 Folkstone Way
West Vancouver
(604) 926-3212

Tojo's Restaurant
#202 – 777 West Broadway
(604) 872-8050

Victoria and Area

Blue Crab Bar and Grill
146 Kingston Street
(250) 480-1999

Deep Cove Chalet
11190 Chalet Road
Sydney
(250) 656-3541

Marina Restaurant
1327 Beach Drive
(250) 598-8555

Pescatore's Fish House
614 Humboldt Street
(250) 385-4512

Sooke Harbour House
1528 Whiffen Spit Road
Sooke
(250) 642-3421

New Brunswick

Moncton and Area

Captain Dan's
Pointe du Chêne Wharf
Pointe du Chêne
(506) 533-2855

Le Chateau a Pàpe
2 Steadman Street South
Moncton
(506) 855-7273

Fisherman's Paradise
Dieppe
(506) 859-4388
Shediac
(506) 532-6811

Maverick's Steak & Lobster House
40 Weldon Street
Moncton
(506) 855-3346

McPhail's Lobster Haven
Rte. 535
Buctouche
(506) 743-8432

St. James Gate
14 Church Street
Moncton
(506) 388-4283

Saint John

Billy's Seafood Fish Market
   and Restaurant
49 – 51 Charlotte Street
City Market
(506) 672-3474

Grannan's
Market Square
(506) 634-1555

Newfoundland

St. John's

Crooked Crab & Savage Lobster
98 Duckworth Street
(709) 738-8900

Seafood Galley
25 Kenmount Road
(709) 753-1255

The Stone House
8 Kenna's Hill
(709) 753-2380

Nova Scotia

Chester

Galley Seaside Restaurant
Rte. 3
(902) 275-4700

The Rope Loft
36 Water Street
(902) 275-3430

Halifax

The Five Fishermen
1740 Argyle Street
(902) 422-4421

McKelvie's
1680 Lower Water Street
(902) 421-6161

O'Carroll's
1860 Upper Water Street
(902) 423-4405

Salty's Bar & Grill
1869 Upper Water Street
(902) 423-6818

Upper Deck
Privateer's Warehouse
3rd Floor
Historic Properties
(902) 422-1289

Mahone Bay

Inlet Café
Rte. 3
(902) 624-6363

Mimi's Ocean Grill
662 South Main Street
(902) 624-1342

Ontario

Toronto

Adriatico Ristorante
14 Dupont Street
(416) 323-7442

Joso's
202 Davenport Road
(416) 925-1903

La Pecherie
133 Yorkville Avenue
(416) 926-9545

Mediterra
133 Richmond Street West
(416) 861-1211

Oyster Boy
872 Queen Street West
(416) 534-3432

Rodney's Oyster House
469 King Street West
(416) 363-8105

Starfish Oyster Bed & Grill
100 Adelaide Street East
(416) 366-7827

Wah Sing Seafood
47 Baldwin Street
(416) 599-8822

Prince Edward Island

Fiddles and Vittles
Seasonal
Cavendish
(902) 963-3003

Fishbones Oyster Bar & Seafood Grill
Seasonal
Charlottetown
Victoria Row
(902) 628-6569

Lobster on the Wharf
Seasonal
Charlottetown
Prince Street at Waterfront Wharf
(902) 368-2888

Lobster Shanty Lounge & Restaurant
Montague
(902) 838-2463

New Glasgow Lobster Supper
Seasonal
Hunter River
(902) 964-2870

St. Ann's Church Lobster Suppers
Seasonal
Hope River
(902) 621-0635

Quebec

Montreal

Chez Delmo
211 rue Notre Dame ouest
(514) 849-4061

Desjardins Kaiko
1175 rue Mackay
(514) 866-9741

Les Halles
1450 rue Crescent
(514) 844-2328

Le Homard Fou
403 Place Jacques Cartier
(514) 398-9090

Maestro S.V.P. Seafood & Oyster Bar
3615 Boulevard St. Laurent
(514) 842-6447

Le Mas des Oliviers
1216 rue Bishop
(514) 861-6733

La Mer
1840 Boul. Rene Levesque est
(514) 522-2889

Chez Pauze
1657 rue St. Catherine ouest
(514) 932-6118

Restaurant du Vieux Port
39 St. Paul est
Old Montreal
(514) 866-3175

IN THE UNITED STATES

California

Monterey

Abalonetti Seafood Trattoria
57 Fisherman's Wharf
(408) 373-1851

Bubba Gump Shrimp Co.
720 Cannery Row
(408) 373-1884

Mike's Seafood Restaurant
25 Fisherman's Wharf #1
(408) 372-6153

Old Fisherman's Grotto
39 Fisherman's Wharf #1
(408) 375-4604

The Sardine Factory
701 Wave Street
(408) 373-3775

The Whaling Station Restaurant
763 Wave Street
(408) 373-3778

Newport Beach

Bluewater Grill Seafood Restaurant
    & Oyster Bar
630 Lido Park Drive
(949) 675-3474

The Crab Cooker
2200 Newport Boulevard
(949) 673-0100

Joe's Crab Shack
2607 West Pacific Coast Highway
(949) 650-1818

Newport Landing Restaurant
   & Oyster Bar
503 East Edgewater Avenue
(949) 675-2373

San Diego

Anthony's Seafood Restaurant
1360 North Harbor Drive
(619) 232-5103

Blue Crab Restaurant
4922 North Harbor Drive
(619) 224-3000

Harbor House Restaurant
831 West Harbor Drive
(619) 232-1141

Joe's Crab Shack
4325 Ocean Boulevard
(858) 274-3474

Lobster Co.
420 E Street
(619) 233-3377

San Francisco

Aqua
252 California Street
(415) 956-9662

Elite Café
2049 Fillmore Street
(415) 346-8668

Farallon Restaurant
450 Post Street
(415) 956-6969

Hayes Street Grill
320 Hayes Street
(415) 863-5545

Plouf
40 Belden Place
(415) 986-6491

Swan Oyster Depot
1517 Polk Street
(415) 673-1101

Tadich Grill
240 California Street
(415) 391-1849

Yabbie's Coastal Kitchen
2237 Polk Street
(415) 474-4088

Connecticut

Greenwich

Elm Street Oyster House
11 West Elm Street
(203) 629-5795

Hartford

No Fish Today
80 Pratt Street
(860) 244-2100

USS Chowder Pot
165 Brainard Road
(860) 244-3311

Stamford

Ocean 211
211 Summer Street
(203) 973-0494

Florida

Fort Lauderdale & Area

Charley's Crab
3000 NE 32nd Avenue
(954) 561-4800

Cami's Seafood Restaurant
7996 Pines Boulevard
Pembroke Pines
(954) 987-3474

Flanigan's Seafood Bar & Grill
1479 East Commercial Boulevard
(954) 493-5329

Hobo's Fish Joint
Palm Springs Plaza
10317 Royal Palm Boulevard
Coral Springs
(954) 346-5484

Old Boston Seafood Company
5353 Sheridan Street
Hollywood
(954) 322-9227

Pines Seafood Grill
10060 Pines Boulevard
Pembroke Pines
(954) 450-4977

Sea Grill Seafood Grill & Bar
2029 Harrison Street
Hollywood
(954) 926-5757

Key West

Crabby Dick's
712 Duval Street
(305) 294-7229

Captain Bob's Grill
2200 North Roosevelt Boulevard
(305) 294-6433

Miami & Area

Garcia's
398 NW North River Drive
(305) 375-0765

Joe's Stone Crab
11 Washington Avenue
Miami Beach
(305) 673-0365

Sarasota & Area

Moore's Stone Crab
800 Broadway Street
Longboat Key
(941) 383-1748

Sassy Snapper
70 Indiana Avenue
North Eaglewood
(941) 475-8975

Georgia

Atlanta

Atlanta Fish Market
265 Pharr Road
(404) 262-3165

Brasserie Le Coze
3393 Peachtree Road
(404) 266-1440

Chops/Lobster Bar
70 W. Paces Ferry Road
(Buckhead Plaze)
(404) 262-2675

Savannah

Bistro Savannah
309 W. Congress Street
(912) 233-6266

The Lady & Sons
311 W. Congress Street
(912) 233-2600

Illinois

Chicago

Atlantique
5101 North Clark Street
(773) 275-9191

Heaven on Seven
3311 North Clark Street
(312) 280-7774

Joe's Seafood, Prime Steak & Stone Crab
60 East Grand Avenue
(312) 379-5637

Louisiana

New Orleans

Arnaud's
813 Bienville Street
(French Quarter)
(504) 523-5433

Bayona
430 Dauphine Street
(504) 525-4455

Commander's Palace
1403 Washington Avenue
(504) 899-8221

K-Paul's Louisiana Kitchen
416 Chartres Street
(French Quarter)
(504) 524-7394

Ralph & Kacoo's
519 Toulouse Street
(French Quarter)
(504) 522-5226

Maine

Freeport

Harraseeket Lobster
Town Landing
(207) 865-3635

Kittery Point

Chauncey Creek Lobster Pound
Chauncey Creek Road
(207) 439-1030

New Harbor

Shaw's Fish and Lobster Wharf
Seasonal
(207) 677-2200

Portland

Fore Street
288 Fore Street
(207) 775-2717

South Thomaston

Waterman's Beach Lobster
Seasonal
Waterman's Beach Road
(207) 596-7819

Tenants Harbor

Cod End
Seasonal
Town Dock
(207) 372-6782

Wiscasset

Red's Eats
Water and Main Streets
(207) 882-6128

Maryland

Baltimore

Charleston Restaurant
1000 Lancaster Street
(410) 332-7373

Obrycki's
Seasonal
1727 East Pratt Street
(410) 732-6399

Rusty Scupper
402 Key Highway
(410) 727-3678

Broomes Island

Stoney's Seafood House
Oyster House Road
(410) 586-1888

St. Michaels

Crab Claw
Navy Point
(410) 745-2900

208 Talbot
208 North Talbot Street
(410) 745-3838

Massachusetts

Boston

KingFish Hall
Faneuil Hall
188 South Market Street
(617) 523-8862

Legal Sea Foods
Prudential Center
800 Boylston Street
(617) 266-6800
*(Plus nine other locations in
and around Boston.)*

McCormick & Schmick's
Park Plaza Hotel
34 Columbus Avenue
(617) 482-3999
Also: Faneuil Hall
North Market Street
(617) 720-5522

Cambridge

East Coast Grill & Raw Bar
1271 Cambridge Street
(617) 491-6568

Jasper White's Summer Shack
149 Alewife Brook Parkway
(617) 520-9500

Cape Cod and Provincetown

Dancing Lobster
373 Commercial Street
(508) 487-0900

Essex

Woodman's of Essex
Rt. 133
Main Street
(978) 768-6057

Martha's Vineyard and Menemsha

Home Port
512 North Road
(508) 645-2679

Nantucket

The SeaGrille
45 Sparks Avenue
(508) 325-5700

Westport

Back Eddy
1 Bridge Road
(508) 636-6500

New Jersey

Cape May

The Merion Inn
106 Decatur Street
(609) 884-8363

Cherry Hill

Bobby Chez
1990 Route 70 East
(856) 751-7373

Highlands

Doris & Ed's
348 Shore Drive
(732) 872-1565

Middletown

Navesink Fishery
1004 Route 36 South
(732) 291-8017

Princeton

Blue Point Grill
258 Nassau Street
(609) 921-1211

Surf City

Yellow Fin
104 Long Beach Boulevard
(609) 494-7001

Trenton

John Henry's Seafood
2 Mifflin Street
(609) 396-3083

New York

New York City

Aquagrill
210 Spring Street
(212) 274-0505

Blue Fin
W Hotel Times Square
1567 Broadway
(212) 918-1400

Blue Water Grill
31 Ubion Square West
(212) 675-9500

Clemente's Maryland Crabhouse
3939 Emmons Avenue
Brooklyn
(718) 646-7373

Esca
402 West 43rd Street
(212) 564-7272

fresh
105 Reade Street
(212) 406-1900

Gage & Tollner
372 Fulton Street
Brooklyn
(718) 875-5181

Le Bernardin
155 West 51st Street
(212) 554-1515

London Lennie's
63 – 88 Woodhaven Boulevard
Queens
(718) 894-8084

Manhattan Ocean Club
57 West 58th Street
(212) 371-7777

Oceana
55 East 54th Street
(212) 759-5941

Oyster Bar at Grand Central
    Grand Central Station
42nd Street and Vanderbilt Avenue
(212) 490-6650

Pearl Oyster Bar
18 Cornelia Street
(212) 691-8211

Sea Grill
Rockefeller Center
19 West 49th Street
(212) 332-7610

The Sea View
636 City Island Avenue
Bronx
(718) 885-9263

Long Island

Bayview Bistro
44 Main Street
Northport
(631) 262-9744

Burke & Shapiro
155 Main Street
Smithtown
(631) 265-3300

Burke & Shapiro
3500 West Sunrise Highway
Wantaugh
(516) 781-3610

Dave's Grill
468 West Lake Drive
Montauk
(631) 668-9190

Fiddleheads
62 South Street
Oyster Bay
(516) 922-2999

Lobster Roll Northside
3225 Sound Avenue
Riverhead
(631) 369-3039

Lobster Roll Southside
1980 Montauk Highway
Amagansett
(631) 267-3740

Nautilus Café
46 Woodcleft Avenue
Freeport
(516) 379-2566

Plaza Café
61 Hill Street
Southampton
(631) 283-9323

Riverbay Seafood
700 Willis Avenue
Williston Park
(516) 742-9191

Saracen
108 Wainscott Stone Road
Wainscott
(631) 537-6255

Ted Milan
36 East Park Avenue
Long Beach
(516) 670-0007

Oregon

Astoria

Cannery Café
1 6th Street
(503) 325-8642

Cannon Beach

The Bistro
263 North Hemlock Street
(503) 436-2661

Doogers
1371 South Hemlock Street
(503) 436-2225

Coos Bay

Portside Restaurant
8001 Kingfisher Road
(541) 888-5544

Newport

Canyon Bay Restaurant & Bookstore
S.W. Canyon Way
(off Bay Front Boulevard)
(541) 265-8319

Whale's Tale
Seasonal
452 S.W. Bay Boulevard
(541) 265-8660

Portland

Jake's Famous Crawfish
401 S.W. 12th Avenue
(503) 226-1419

Winterborn
3520 N.E. 42nd Avenue
(503) 249-8486

Pennsylvania

Philadelphia

Dmitri's
795 S. Third Street
(215) 625-0556

Dmitri's
2227 Pine Street
(215) 985-3680

Striped Bass
1500 Walnut Street
(215) 732-4444

Rhode Island

Newport

Black Pearl
Bannister's Wharf
(401) 846-5264

Flo's Clam Shack
4 Wave Avenue
(401) 847-8141

Scales & Shells
527 Thames Street
(401) 848-9378

South Carolina

Charleston

Carolina's
10 Exchange Street
(843) 724-3800

Peninsula Grill
112 North Market Street
(843) 723-0700

The Wreck
106 Haddrell Street
Mount Pleasant
(843) 884-0052

Myrtle Beach

Sea Captain's House
3002 North Ocean Boulevard
(843) 448-8082

Texas

Dallas

Nick & Sam's
3008 Maple Avenue
(214) 871-7444

Galveston

Fisherman's Wharf
3901 Avenue O
(409) 765-5708

Saltwater Grill
2017 Post Office Street
(409) 726-3474

Houston

Pesce
3029 Kirby Drive
(713) 522-4858

Washington

Seattle

Anthony's Pier 66
2201 Alaskan Way
(206) 448-6688

Flying Fish
2234 1st Avenue
(206) 728-8595

Elliott's Oyster House
1201 Alaskan Way
Pier 56
(206) 623-4340

Etta's Seafood
2020 Western Avenue
(206) 443-6000

Oceanaire Seafood Room
1700 Seventh Avenue
(206) 267-2277

Waterfront Seafood Grill
2801 Alaskan Way
Pier 70
(206) 956-9171

Good Places to Eat Shellfish

The Authors

Marjorie Harris was born on the Prairies which explains her uncontrollable yearning for all forms of shellfish. She has written 14 books on gardening, is the Editor-in-Chief of *Gardening Life* magazine and keeps shells all over her garden as mementos of all her great shellfish experiences.

Peter Taylor was born in New Brunswick on Canada's East Coast and claims to have never passed an oyster bar without popping in for a dozen oysters and a pint or two. He has written nine books — his latest two, *Three Bricks Shy of a Load*, and *Dumb Men & the Women Who Love Them* are both published by Fitzhenry & Whiteside.